D1004199

Small Group Facilitation: Improving Process and Performance in Groups and Teams

Judith A. Kolb

HRD Press • Amherst • Massachusetts

Published by: HRD Press, Inc.
                22 Amherst Road
                Amherst, MA 01002
                413-253-3488
                800-822-2801 (U.S. and Canada)
                413-253-3490 (fax)
                www.hrdpress.com

ISBN 978-1-59996-228-3

Editorial services by Sally M. Farnham
Production services by Jean S. Miller
Cover design by Eileen Klockars

~ Contents ~

Contents

Contents

~ **Preface** ~

Just about everything we do in organizations to at least some degree revolves around groups and teams. Most likely we are a member of a work group, unit, or team. If that is not the case, we attend meetings—perhaps many meetings. Groups are everywhere. And, outside the organization, groups are increasingly used as vehicles for organizing action for a cause, personal support, medical information exchange, or discussion of shared topics of interest. All these groups are systems within systems and affected by variables both internal and external, positive and negative.

Of course these groups do not always work as planned. Sometimes everything goes right, and a group marches on with hardly a blip toward its desired outcome. Others experience a few bumps along the way, but manage to succeed in the end. Still others have significant things go wrong that cause group members to lose focus. Many factors make a difference in the success or failure of groups. This book focuses on one of the most important—group process. The process focus of small group facilitation helps groups move more efficiently toward their goals. Whether we are talking about routine meetings, steering committees, communities of practice, learning groups, or long-term work teams, facilitation has a role.

The demand for facilitation services today is an indication of the importance of this role. Groups often work under tight deadlines and with reduced resources. Having the best possible process is a way to allow group members to focus on the task at hand and the very real problems and issues they face. The goal of this book is to help facilitators help groups achieve desired outcomes.

Organization and Features

Small Group Facilitation: Improving Process and Performance in Groups and Teams is designed around a research-based Framework for Facilitation that provides support for the practical suggestions, tools, strategies, and techniques presented throughout the book.

The book consists of three parts: Overview; Framework for Facilitation, and Techniques for Decision Making, Problem Solving, and Strategic Planning. The two chapters in Part One provide an introduction to small group facilitation and a discussion of how groups work. Part Two discusses in detail the eight elements of the Framework for Facilitation: planning and organization, communication, task, relationships and climate, values and ethics, conflict, creativity, and techniques. Part Three focuses on techniques and gives an expanded explanation and description of 17 techniques, including four variations of brainstorming. Each technique follows the following format: name and brief description, references, use, materials needed, advantages, disadvantages, comments/suggestions, and steps and/or an example.

Every chapter begins with a bulleted list of Key Concepts, ends with a Summary and a listing of References, and includes relevant research and practical suggestions along with many of my own experiences in facilitating groups. Some of the details of my experiences have been changed to respect confidentiality, but the lessons learned remain evident. Examples of group dialogues and/or tools and procedures ready for application are presented for each element in the framework. Although this book is not meant to be an exhaustive review of research in small groups and facilitation, studies that relate directly to chapter content are included. Chapter 2, in particular, contains a wealth of information on how groups work. My intent in developing this book was to provide material that will be of practical use for people currently involved with or interested in small group facilitation.

Techniques from a variety of sources and fields of study are included in the last three chapters. Each technique is presented in its entirety and can be used as a full approach or modified as you see fit. I suggest that you take the best or most useful pieces from a variety of techniques and create hybrid techniques that suit your groups and your personal style of facilitation.

Audience

Anyone who works with groups or is interested in improving the effectiveness of groups should find value in this book. A partial list follows:

- ❖ facilitators
- ❖ group members
- ❖ leaders and managers
- ❖ trainers
- ❖ mediators
- ❖ faculty members
- ❖ human resource managers
- ❖ human resource development consultants
- ❖ organization development consultants
- ❖ coaches
- ❖ counselors
- ❖ school administrators

Suggestions for Use

Although this book was designed to be read from beginning to end, and I encourage you to take this approach, I realize that some readers might be drawn to specific chapters. If, for example, your group has problems with communication and is experiencing a great deal of conflict, you might want to turn first to those chapters. Each chapter in this book makes sense on its own, although each also builds on or relates to other chapters. Chapter 3 explains how all eight elements in the Framework for Facilitation are connected.

~ Acknowledgments ~

I acknowledge and appreciate the contributions, talents, and patience of three colleagues who have influenced my thinking on small groups: the late Alvin Goldberg from the University of Denver; Carl Larson, also from the University of Denver; and Dennis Gouran from Pennsylvania State University. Thank you.

Several of my research studies cited in this book, in the field of facilitation and in the wider field of groups, were collaborative. I want to thank my coauthors: Barbara Gray, Sungmi Jin, William Rothwell, Louise Sandmeyer, and Ji Hoon Song. Additional thanks go to Jin Yong Kim and Jin Gu Lee for their help in assembling the figures for this book.

In a more general but equally heartfelt way, I thank the numerous students in my team seminars, workshops, and small group facilitation classes over the years. The discussions in these groups have led to insights, reflections, and "aha" moments that have improved my competencies as a facilitator as well as given me much laughter and occasional tears. Stories from these classes, told mostly by people working in the field, have made me realize just how committed facilitators are to helping groups and the individuals in groups have good experiences. My hat is off to you all. To the groups and teams I've worked with over the years, I appreciate your collegiality and your willingness to try a variety of approaches and techniques. Several of the suggestions for use and modification of techniques that appear in the last section of this book emerged from these sessions.

Publication of a book involves many people. I am grateful to Robert Carkhuff, Sally Farnham, and the team at HRD Press for their efforts and expertise in bringing this book to print.

Lastly, I thank my family for their unwavering love, support, and encouragement. I dedicate this book to my parents, Floyd and Virginia, who share my love of reading.

Part One
Overview

Introduction to Small Group Facilitation

Key Concepts

- Definition of facilitation
- Process facilitation vs. dual role facilitation
- Types of groups and teams
- Why groups are important

With today's organizational emphasis on teamwork, there is an increasing interest in and need for small group facilitation. Think of the number of meetings or other group sessions you've participated in over the past few months. Were they well organized? Were relevant issues raised? Did group members appear engaged in the discussions? Did you leave feeling a sense of accomplishment? If so, chances are that the person in charge of planning and running the session had some knowledge of the principles of small group facilitation. Some meetings are relatively easy—an individual with organization skills, a sense of how to get people to work well together, and a memory of past group experiences (good, bad, and ugly) should be able to avoid the pitfalls that make group sessions memorable for all the wrong reasons. Even so-called easy meetings, however, can benefit from the skills brought by a process expert who is trained to handle issues that arise in groups and who knows a variety of techniques that are useful in helping participants make decisions and solve problems. And, of course, many of us have been in a routine meeting that changed in a heartbeat to one that challenged the skills of the leader and the patience of everyone in attendance. The sheer volume of group meetings today and the need for these sessions to run smoothly and productively are the reasons why facilitation skills are in demand.

3

What Is Facilitation?

Facilitation is one of those words that has multiple meanings, all of them valid. People called in to facilitate a group may be expected to lead, train, present new information, make process suggestions, mediate, or perhaps serve in a combination of these roles. The focus of this book is on the group process role, with the realization that people who perform this function may also be expected to fulfill other roles. Group process focuses on the way in which a group goes about accomplishing its purpose. Details regarding that purpose or the actual decisions made by the group are of interest to the facilitator only in relationship to the process or functioning of the group.

The word "facilitate" comes from the Latin word for "to make easy." Frey (1994, p. 4) offers this definition of facilitation, "any meeting technique, procedure, or practice that makes it easier for groups to interact and/or accomplish their goals." Thus, the job of the small group facilitator is to make the group's task easier—to help a group accomplish its purpose by using appropriate and functional process. The following definition of a small group process facilitator adapted from Kolb, Jin, and Song (2008) captures the essence of this role:

> a person who remains neutral in the actual decision(s) of the group but who assumes the responsibility for managing the group's process while it is attempting to identify and discuss issues, build commitment, solve a problem, reach a decision, or perform a task (p. 123).

Neutrality is important in order that the facilitator's focus remain on the process, not the outcome. A process facilitator should not be personally concerned about the issues under discussion by the group nor have a vested interest in the outcome. Too much involvement with issues and decisions is distracting and might consciously or unconsciously affect procedural choices made by the facilitator. When someone serves a dual function such as facilitator/content matter expert, facilitator/trainer, facilitator/mediator, or leader/ facilitator, that distinction should be made clear to all involved.

Purpose of Facilitation

Assuming then that the facilitator is neutral, what does "managing the group's process" mean? You may have heard the term, "group dynamics," which Brilhart (1986) defines as "a field of inquiry concerned with the nature of small groups, including how they develop and interact, and their relationships with individuals, other groups, and institutions" (p. 3). Relationships among group members, particularly cohesion among group members, is at the heart of group dynamics theory as conceptualized by Kurt Lewin in the 1940s (Lewin, 1948). Managing the group's process involves also managing group relationships. Although groups and teams are prevalent today, members of these groups do not automatically know how to work well together. A facilitator will help groups with both task and relationship functions or, in other words, help them accomplish their task and get along with each other.

Short-term/extended facilitation. Often a facilitator is hired for a short-term task-oriented facilitation that involves only one meeting or perhaps a series of meetings held close together in time. The facilitator's role in this case is to help the group achieve the desired task outcome while monitoring and managing group climate and relationships. The facilitator is not present to teach, although members might retain some knowledge about group process that will help them in future meetings. The purpose in short-term facilitation is to get the job done. The facilitator takes primary responsibility for managing the group's process and temporarily improves the process while doing so. Schwartz (2002) contrasts this basic type of facilitation with developmental facilitation. In the latter, the facilitator helps the group develop process skills, and over time, members are able to manage their own process without the aid of a facilitator. In another form of extended long-term facilitation, development of process skills is a secondary goal. The primary responsibility for managing group process remains, by group choice, with the facilitator. These distinctions have process implications. If group members know each other and have worked together for some time, they will have established ways of working that will influence decisions made by the facilitator. Likewise, as a facilitator works with people over an extended period of time, they become comfortable with each other; this also influences group process decisions and functions.

Facilitator/facilitation. Although the focus of this book is primarily on facilitation as performed by one person or perhaps cofacilitators serving in the traditional role of managing group process, I realize that facilitation skills are valuable for anyone who leads discussions or regularly works with people in group situations. The content covered in this book is presented in a way that should be useful to facilitators, trainers, human resource development and organization development consultants, managers, coaches, mediators, teachers, social workers, and people working in just about any profession you can name. Individuals who find themselves serving as group members may also want to learn how to improve the group's process, if for no other reason than to reduce the time they spend in meetings. My suggestions to facilitators throughout this book are directed toward whatever person or persons have assumed the facilitation role.

Much of what we do today involves issues discussed, relationships formed, tasks performed, and decisions made by individuals working in small groups. Improvement in the functioning of these groups is of primary interest to people who work on or with them and those whose work or personal activities are affected by group efforts or outputs—in short, just about everyone.

Dual Roles

Process improvement is the primary role of a small group facilitator, but this role may be combined with other responsibilities. As a facilitator, you could be hired to serve a dual role. If that happens, you need to clarify expectations for your role and communicate to group members when you are serving as a process facilitator and when you are moving into a different role. And, of course, you need to consider whether it is possible for you to function effectively in both roles. The first dual role is one of the easiest to accomplish.

Facilitator/content matter expert. In this role, you are brought in as an expert in some area of content in addition to group process. Perhaps you have experience with a particular system or practice that a group is considering adopting or a background in helping organizations comply with safety regulations or employment laws. In these cases, you have no direct interest in actual decisions the group makes, but you have information above and beyond your knowledge of group process, and you should expect to be called upon to provide content guidance. These roles work together quite well as long as you do not benefit directly from the group decision. For example, if you are selling a particular computer software, you should not also serve as the process facilitator. The process decisions you make to help the group reach a decision might influence the outcome of that decision. The next role is also quite common. With group discussion playing a major role in the establishment of a participatory learning climate, someone with facilitation skills will find training a complementary activity.

Facilitator/trainer. Your primary role here is to facilitate group member learning in an area of content. The expectation is that the training will be highly interactive, with knowledge gain as the goal. You may, for example, be asked to talk about teamwork. In such cases, you would incorporate actual training modules on aspects of teamwork as you work with the group to improve its process. Usually the participants will be from an intact working group or team. On occasion, however, they represent a variety of teams and will be carrying information back to their work units. In the latter case, you are training the trainer. Usually a facilitator/trainer provides instruction on group-related issues while also working with the group to improve its process. There is a wider application of this role, however. As more and more information sharing is done electronically, face-to-face training sessions incorporate group work, discussions, and activities rather than presentations by the trainer. Someone working as a trainer today in a variety of content areas and contexts might be considered a trainer/ facilitator. The next combined role is less common than the first two and requires extensive experience in conflict resolution.

Facilitator/mediator. In this application of the facilitation role, the group in question has some significant issues that require the services of a mediator. Usually the person brought in for this role has extensive training and/or certification in mediation. The questions that are covered later in this book (Chapter 4) should help you determine whether your background and skills are sufficient for the job in question. Always probe for additional detail when a conflict situation is mentioned and don't hesitate to refer this to someone else if you believe you aren't qualified. I remember receiving a phone call from someone who started off by saying he had heard that I had experience in working with groups in conflict. After asking a series of questions, I determined that the group situation he described went beyond what I was comfortable handling. I then referred him to someone who specialized in mediation. Each of us needs to make these decisions for ourselves, but asking questions about expectations is important if we are to achieve the goal of helping the group. I now turn to the last of the four dual roles covered in this chapter. The role of leader/ facilitator is, in my opinion, the most challenging of the four.

Leader/facilitator. In this situation, you are considered the leader of the group. This may be an official position, such as being the manager or boss, or a less official but nonetheless designated role as leader of a project. In any case, members view you as a leader and will expect you to have opinions on the issues under discussion. You are not neutral in decision making. You might notice in this last role that the order of the terms are reversed. While the other combined roles are listed as facilitator/content matter expert, facilitator/trainer, and facilitator/mediator, this final role reverses the order. The role of leader takes precedence over any other. I'm using leader/ facilitator here to describe someone in a leadership role who wants to encourage group members, who may be direct reports (subordinates), to take on more responsibility for decision making.

A discussion of the purpose and intent of a meeting or group session is crucial in all situations but especially vital on occasions that involve leader/facilitators. When you are the boss, members are concerned about their relationships with you and also about the security of their jobs. Do not expect the openness that might occur in discussions that are led by a process facilitator. However, this combined role can still be productive. Group members who believe you to be sincere in your desire to facilitate an open discussion of issues that involve everyone most likely will be willing and even eager to participate. Be sure to clarify the members' role in decision making. If they expect to have an equal voice in a decision and they find out later that the decision they made was ignored, they will justifiably feel frustrated and hesitant to participate in the future. If, however, they are told that the leader wants input from them that will be considered when the decision is made, expectations and decision-making parameters are clear.

As groups become more involved in decision making, leaders who have skills in understanding and improving group functioning might also find themselves better able to relate to individuals inside and outside the group context. Listening skills, in particular, are valuable to anyone in a leadership or facilitation role.

Other. You might perform another combination of roles. Coach/facilitator is one. Although I doubt that most athletic coaches would describe themselves as facilitators, anyone who can convince a team that is behind at half-time to come out and turn a game around definitely has the ability to motivate a group to accomplish a goal. Coaches work in all types of organizational settings outside the athletic arena and use many of the same skills as facilitators. Counselors, too, work in group settings, as do human resource professionals. Much of what we do today, we do in groups.

Types of Groups

In this book, I use the term "groups" to refer to both groups and teams, although I realize the distinction between the two. Both are collections of individuals who share some common interests and goals and who perceive themselves, for at least a short period of time, to be a unit. A facilitated session might involve people who come together for one specific purpose and who may never meet again as a group after accomplishing that purpose. Teams, generally, refer to long-term groups that have defined goals requiring mutual cooperation and dependence. Groups and teams exist for a variety of reasons. The following list and descriptions should give you a good idea of the purposes for which individuals form groups. Although most of the groups listed are found primarily in organizational or business contexts, others occur in a variety of settings. All use facilitators at one point or another. Keep in mind that organizations differ in the labels they give to groups and teams. As a facilitator, the purpose of the group is more important to you than the name used.

Task force groups are formed to bring together individuals who have specific specialties that are needed to accomplish a designated task or project. A task force might be formed to investigate how to restructure an organizational unit or to recommend changes in a current procedure. Task forces are given distinct responsibilities and a time frame within which to conclude the job.

Steering committees resemble task force groups in that a variety of individuals with differing skill sets and backgrounds come together for a specific purpose. The goal, however, is implementation rather than idea generation. If, for example, a task force recommends a specific change, a steering committee might be formed to implement that change.

Focus groups are a collection of individuals brought together to concentrate on an issue or a topic. Early use of focus groups was for advertising and marketing purposes: members were asked to react to commercials, test products, or otherwise help organizations target their products to desired customers. In a similar way, focus groups are used by political campaigns to try out slogans and campaign rhetoric. Current use has expanded to include any group that is brought together for a short time (usually one session) to give reactions to specific organizational or community issues.

Special interest groups. Several types are included here:

- *Social support groups* have few formal task responsibilities but exist rather for the purpose of offering social support to people who find themselves in similar situations or who have common interests. Organizational employees who have returned to school to complete degrees, people serving as caretakers to elderly parents, and individuals facing long-term illnesses or chronic conditions are examples of such groups. Helpful information may be distributed and content matter experts invited, but the primary purpose of these groups is to provide a supportive climate in which mutual concerns may be discussed.

- *Communities of practice* are also springing up in a variety of organizations. These groups are formed around a common interest, as in social support groups, but they have knowledge exchange as a primary purpose. Individuals who have an interest in a specific topic such as informal learning come together to share information, resources, and experience.

- *Community action groups* consist of individuals who are drawn together because of a specific issue such as a change in land use or redistricting of a school district. If the issue has relevance to an organization, members may attend to represent organizational interests. Such groups may be quite large, and membership may vary from one session to another.

Routine meetings of managers, work units, or governance groups are generally held on a set schedule for the purpose of coordinating efforts, discussing issues, making decisions, and allocating resources. **Strategic planning sessions** or retreats provide an opportunity for members of a unit or committee to devote a more extended period of time to an examination of long-range goals and/or other issues that are significant for the functioning of the group.

Board meetings. Boards vary in size and function, but generally are mandated groups of individuals who are charged with the authority to make decisions for people they represent. Some boards have specific policy-making duties and legal responsibilities; others simply recommend policy.

Learning sessions. Training in many topics in organizations has long involved substantial amounts of group work. The training session itself, generally 15 to 20 people, functions as a small group. As learning becomes increasingly interactive, people who lead workshops serve more as facilitators and resource people than as lecturers or traditional instructors. The issues faced, particularly in helping people work well together, are similar to those in other work groups.

Online/web-based groups. Many groups today use technology to connect with members. The groups mentioned earlier may incorporate aspects of online participation as well as face-to-face meetings to accomplish group tasks. Some groups may meet totally online. Although the assumption in this book is that most facilitated groups involve a significant face-to-face component, much of the material discussed can be adapted for online use.

Types of Teams

Facilitators who have an interest and background in team training or consulting may work with a variety of types of work teams. This could involve training members on specific communication or relationship skills needed within the team or expanding the process focus to include work environment factors or performance issues.

- *Primary work teams* consist of individuals who work together on a regular basis in a unit that generally consists of peers and a supervisor. This is the individual's home base or primary place of work. The needs of these teams vary according to the tasks involved.

- *Project teams* consist of shorter term projects that have specific goals such as the design of a new product or implementation of a new process. Individuals may work on more than one project team or may be a member of a primary work team as well as a shorter term project team.

- *Self-managing teams* are units formed with the purpose of having individual team members share management responsibilities. Self-managing teams generally schedule their own work, cross-train members, monitor work processes, conduct internal evaluations, and assess and improve their own processes.

- Teams devoted to *quality improvement* began after World War II when Edward Deming introduced his quality control methods to Japanese workers. Currently, in the United States and elsewhere, a variety of organizational frameworks using the word *quality* provide support for teams pursuing improvement in products, process, and procedures.

Kaizen teams are similar to self-managing teams in that they are concerned with incremental, continuous improvement. "*Kaizen*, translated from the Japanese, is composed of *kai* 'change' and *zen* 'good' (Stone, 2010, p. 64). The activities providing the opportunity for improvement to occur are referred to as *kaizen events.*

Since teams are always groups but the reverse is not true, I will use *groups* as the generic term for both throughout this book.

Why Groups Are Important

There is a movement toward increased use of groups within organizations of all types, in communities and schools, and by individuals with common interests or needs who are banding together for support. The popularity of Internet support groups is one indication of this need for community (Alexander, Peterson, & Hollingshead, 2003). LaFasto and Larson (2001) talk about factors providing impetus for this movement:

> We believe that the movement toward teamwork and collaboration is shaped by two societal forces. It is *driven* by the need to find new and more effective ways of dealing with complex problems. It *is made possible* by the increasing social capacities of individual and collectives to use collaborative strategies when dealing with common problems (p. xx).

This statement poses both an opportunity and a challenge for small group facilitators. Although our goal is to help groups and teams work together more efficiently and thus improve the capacity to use collaborative strategies, we also realize the difficulty of this task. Groups differ widely in the efficacy of their processes and the success of their outcomes. We hear people groan when they are assigned to yet another group. Problems with group work and the frustrations many people feel when sitting in weekly meetings are regular topics in office-based cartoons and story lines. Sayings such as "A camel is a work designed by committee" and "A committee is a body that keeps minutes and wastes hours" have been around for a long time; I'm sure you can think of others. Whenever I mention the topic of facilitation and explain what it involves, I almost always hear some version of, "I spend most of my week in meetings." The tone of voice used when making these statements does not lead me to believe that people are happy with this use of their time.

Yet we also know the power of groups and teams when they are working well. Most of us have been part of groups that made a difference: instances where we felt that each member contributed skills and talents to a joint effort that allowed the group to achieve something special. Michaelson, Watson, and Black (1989) found that group decision making outperformed that of their best member 97 percent of the time. This does not mean that groups are always preferred over individual effort. Assume there is a problem with technology that is understood only by people with certain skills. If you have access to an individual who has the requisite skill set, that one person may be all you need.

But as the problems we face become more complicated and move beyond what can be fixed by one individual, however talented, harnessing the power of group work becomes even more important. Groups that work well together have **synergy:** the sum of the combined effort of all members working together is greater than the total of the efforts of the individual members. This something extra—this added boost—comes from interaction among the members and the multiple perspectives and increased knowledge brought to bear on the problem, task, or situation involved.

One of the desired outcomes of this book is to help groups move away from the negative perceptions related to wasted time and lack of purpose toward the more positive perceptions of synergy. Effective facilitation plays a large role in this outcome.

Summary

This chapter has covered the definition of facilitation, ways in which process facilitation differs from dual role facilitation, a number of types of groups that you might encounter, and a discussion of why groups are important. Chapter 2 presents some basic information about how groups function and provides context for group process.

References

Alexander, S. C., Peterson, J. L., & Hollingshead, A. B. (2003). Help is at your keyboard: Support groups on the Internet. In. L. R. Frey (Ed.), *Group communication in context* (2nd ed.; pp. 309-334). Mahwah, NJ: Lawrence Erlbaum Associates.

Brilhart, J. K. (1986). *Effective group discussion*. Dubuque, IA: Wm. C. Brown.

Frey, L. R. (1994). Introduction: Applied communication research in group facilitation in natural settings. In. L. R. Frey (Ed.), *Innovations in group facilitation: Applications in natural settings* (pp. 1–26). Cresskill, NJ: Hampton Press.

Kolb, J. A., Jin, S., & Song, J. (2008). A model of small group facilitator competencies. *Performance Improvement Quarterly, 21*(2), 119–133.

LaFasto, F., & Larson, C. (2001). *When teams work best: 6,000 team members and leaders tell what it takes to succeed.* Thousand Oaks, CA: Sage.

Lewin, K. (1948). *Resolving social conflicts.* New York: Harper.

Michaelson, L. K., Watson, W. E., & Black, R. H. (1989). A realistic test of individual vs. group consensus decision making. *Journal of Applied Psychology, 74,* 834–839.

Schwartz, R. (2002). *The skilled facilitator* (Rev. ed.). San Francisco, CA: Jossey-Bass.

Stone, K. B. (2010). Kaizen teams: Integrated HRD practices for successful team building. *Advances in Developing Human Resources, 12*(1), 61–77.

How Groups Work

Key Concepts

- Groups as an open system
- Organizational and outcome variables
- Nature of collaboration
- Tasks and relationship aspects of groups

Although groups exist in many formats and for a variety of purposes, there are some similarities in how groups of all types function. From the vast literature on the nature and functioning of groups, I have chosen to discuss in this chapter those factors of group work that have a strong connection with the process role of facilitation. I start with a discussion of the group as an open system.

Groups as an Open System

An open system "interacts with its environment and transforms resource inputs into outputs" (Schermerhorn, 1984, p. G10). Today's interpretation of open systems realizes the complexity of the global economy, the rapidity of change within organizations, and the increasing need for everyone, and every group or unit, within an organization to adapt. A group is an evolving open system with interactions to and from the group and its external environment flowing between permeable borders. Most systems have limits to their openness, but systems theory makes the clear point that groups do not operate in isolation. Group process can be considered the linking pin or transformational process by which group inputs are transformed into group outputs. However effective the process and the facilitator, group success or outcome depends in large part on how input and process interact. The inputs-process-outputs nature of groups is displayed in Figure 2-1.. The external environment consists of the organization plus factors such as economic conditions, societal issues and restraints, and other influences stemming from society in general. Components of inputs and outcomes, as well as facilitator influence on these components, are discussed following the figure. Variables affecting group process, the middle position of the diagram, are discussed throughout this book.

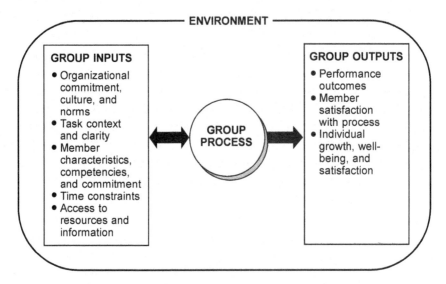

Figure 2-1. The Group as an Open System

Group Inputs

Any aspect of the organizational or external environment, as well as characteristics of individual members, can influence groups. In developing Figure 2-1, I focused on the variables that most often have been identified as crucial factors affecting groups and, from those, the ones that are relevant for the variety of types of groups that involve the services of facilitators. Five components of inputs are covered here: organizational commitment, culture, and norms; task context and clarity; member characteristics, competencies, and commitment; time constraints; and access to resources and information. Support for these components have been reported by a number of researchers (Hackman, 1990; Hirokawa & Keyton, 1995; Kolb, 1996b; Kolb & Sandmeyer, 2008; Larson & LaFasto, 1989). Although time, resources, and information could be considered aspects of organizational commitment, these three are cited so consistently as crucial components that I am mentioning them separately. All are relevant regardless of whether the group is meeting as a one-time special issue group or as a continuing work team, although the importance of each varies according to context.

Organizational commitment, culture, and norms. Commitment refers to how much management cares about the group's purpose; how integral is it to the overall purpose of the organization. The culture of the organization can be defined as what is valued, which usually means what is measured and evaluated. These values may reference internal processes such as support for diversity, teamwork, shared decision making, or creativity or may be stated in terms of commitments to excellence, customer service, or quality. The extent to which these values are reflected in the company's policies and procedures is an indication of the extent to which they are imbedded in the culture of the company. As one example, companies that mention teamwork as a norm and also include assessments of one's ability to work on a team as part of employment decisions and performance reviews can be viewed as having a strong commitment to the value of teamwork.

Norms of behavior are unwritten behaviors, rules, or ways of doing things that develop over time. Common organizational norms range from degrees of formality (use of titles, the way people dress, decoration of offices) to how competitive employees are in closing a sale or making a deal. Groups develop their own norms, but they are influenced by the norms of the organization. If you facilitate a group session with individuals who are used to a norm of creativity, for example, expect considerable resistance if you suggest a very linear problem-solving approach.

Likewise, if shared decision making runs contrary to organizational culture and norms, group members will question the impact of their participation in such a group.

Task context and clarity. Task context refers to the type of group and how the charge or purpose of the group relates to other structures within the organization in terms of hierarchy (influence of the group), linkages to other initiatives and groups, and whether the task is part of the member's general workload, an additional responsibility, or a voluntary contribution of time. Clarity of the specific task or charge is generally assumed, but in truth, confusion about the group's goal is quite common. Can management and members clearly state the purpose of the group in one sentence? Clarifying the expected task, what is needed to accomplish the task, and exactly what outcome is expected are critical issues that are well under the aegis of a facilitator.

Member characteristics, competencies, and commitment. The following questions provide a starting point:

- Do members possess the knowledge, skills, and abilities necessary to complete this task?
- Is everyone who needs to be a part of the team included?
- Are there enough members but not too many?

Desired size of the group varies according the purpose. For decision-making purposes, the group should be only as large as necessary to ensure that all important aspects of the decision or problem are covered by the expertise of the members. A typical range for facilitated groups is 7 to 25 members. For discussion of issues and building commitment, group membership might be as large as 40, although a facilitator would need to incorporate small group discussions within this larger group to encourage full involvement of participants. If members have little experience working in groups, the facilitator may suggest a dual facilitator/trainer role so that time can be spent in developing members' skills in group interactions and decision making.

Member commitment is influenced to a large degree by whether participation is required, requested, or voluntary. Required participation might be a motivating factor if the person is flattered to be considered integral to the group. At other times, however, forced participation, as one might expect, has a negative effect on commitment. Commitment also might be influenced by the history of the issue—how many similar task forces have been convened previously, what happened to the suggestions of those groups, were they generally thought effective or a waste of time? If during your preliminary questions about a group, you hear things that cause you to question member commitment, broach this issue prior to any scheduled facilitated session. Having a group composed of members who resent being there is definitely a challenge.

Time constraints. What is the life cycle of this group? Is it one day, a month, several months, or is it a long-term work group? Many process decisions, as well as possible outcomes, are determined by this factor. Members having the time to meet, as well as a commitment to devoting this time, also falls here.

Access to resources and information. For resources, access generally depends on issues related to task context and commitment. An organization may assign people to task forces and other types of groups without giving them the resources necessary to accomplish the task. This could stem from a lack of knowledge or awareness of group needs, which is easily remedied, or from other reasons that are not as easily addressed. Perhaps the task force was appointed for political reasons (for example, an organization's need to demonstrate commitment to an issue) and does not really have the support of top management. A more positive interpretation may be that the organization wants the group to succeed but time and resources are both in limited supply. Doing more with less is a way of life in many organizations today.

Lack of information could have a more involved explanation tied to power or confidentiality issues. We've all heard the statement, "information is power." People involved in forming the group or in helping it get started may be reluctant to provide full access to information—perhaps a supervisor believes that she/he should be the only one who is fully informed or perhaps the information is confidential. This leads to fundamental questions that should be asked when groups are formed. Is this task better done by a group or an individual? And, if it is better done by a group, do the people in the group have the information and the authority needed to make the decision?

Facilitator's influence on organizational variables. A facilitator who works with a group or with a number of groups in one organization over time has more influence over organizational variables than someone who is brought in for a one-time session. Keeping that difference in mind, the facilitator generally has the most influence in clarifying the task and desired outcome of the group and planning for a particular session or project. See Exhibit 2-1.

Exhibit 2-1
Essential Facilitator Input

❖ Focus of the session

❖ Desired outcome

❖ Time allotment

❖ Format (all day, two half-days)

❖ Location, room arrangement, resources

Asking questions is essential preparation for a facilitated session. At the very least, the facilitator can give feedback if the time allotted to a specific session or sessions is deemed insufficient to accomplish the stated goals. In my experience, people bringing in facilitators to work with groups may be overly ambitious in their determination of what can be accomplished

in one half-day session or during a series of two-hour meetings. In like manner, planners may underestimate a reasonable
timetable for a project. Having too little time for the task
reduces the motivation of members and needs to be addressed.

In some situations involving larger collaborative projects,
the facilitator may be involved in decisions related to the number of people involved in various stages. Many questions asked
during initial consultations on the nature of the groups will
help raise issues essential to planning effective facilitation. If it
appears, for example, that people who have information necessary to the group are not included, that point can be mentioned.
Resource situations may not be apparent until the group is
under way, but decisions about availability of suitable meeting
rooms and necessary technology can be made early in the
process. Facilitators can, and should, probe to get as much
information as possible about the nature and history of a
group. General rhetoric may indicate that an organization is
committed to a group, whereas failure to devote adequate time
and resources gives the opposite impression. Although level of
organizational commitment likely cannot be changed, the
facilitator can point out problems inherent in insufficient time
and resources that may cause a rethinking of the nature of a
project. Organizational culture and norms generally are
beyond the scope of what a facilitator can change—understanding culture and norms, however, provides information
that helps determine an approach to assist a group accomplish
its task. Questions related to these inputs and other issues that
are important in the planning and organization of facilitation
are covered in Chapter 4.

Special relevance for decision making. Several of the components listed under input are closely related to four fundamental assumptions about members of decision-making and
problem-solving groups. Namely, members:

1. want to make an appropriate choice,
2. understand their task and its requirements,

3. have access to necessary resources like information and time, and
4. possess the capabilities and skills needed to deal with various facets of the task and the process required to successfully complete it.

(Gouran & Hirokawa, 2003, p. 29)

Although these assumptions were originally proposed as ideal characteristics of members, today considerable research support exists to consider the assumptions to be a fair description of the needs of members in functional working groups.

Group Outputs/Outcomes

Group outputs or outcomes have traditionally been measured using three criteria: task performance, member satisfaction with group process, and individual member growth and well-being (Albanese, Franklin, & Wright, 1997; Hackman, 1990; Hirokawa & Keyton, 1995; McCaskey, 1979). You will note in Figure 2-1 that "satisfaction" has been included with "growth" and "well-being" on the third factor. I explain reasons for this in the section below.

Although work teams generally have performance standards against which the group's outcome can be measured, other types of groups mentioned in Chapter 1 may or may not have such standards. To the extent possible, facilitators should try to specify up front the measures that will be used to measure success. Let's consider a group working on a strategic planning document. Perhaps their goal is to incorporate information submitted by other groups into a document that is formatted in a certain way by a specific date. Date and format criteria are easy to measure. Either the group does or does not complete the properly formatted document by the deadline. However, the extent to which they successfully and satisfactorily incorporate feedback from other groups is less clear cut. A common procedure is to send rough drafts to individuals or groups who submitted information and ask them to respond by a certain date with any changes or questions about the text. In this manner, adding step upon step, a strategic plan is completed and considered satisfactory. A longer term measure, of course, is the extent to which suggestions and proposals included in the strategic plan are incorporated. Thus, performance can have short-term and long-term aspects. The essential point is that groups that have a clear task purpose should know the measures of performance that will be used to judge successful completion of that task.

In staying with this same example, members of the strategic planning committee may be asked the extent to which they are satisfied with the group process used to accomplish this task. This is the process satisfaction aspect of group outcome.

If you've ever participated in strategic planning, you will know that members are usually just happy they finished by the deadline. If they did not finish, that does not necessarily mean that they were dissatisfied with their process. Perhaps they believed that their process was efficient and that the reasons for not finishing were beyond their control. Task accomplishment and process satisfaction are not always linked.

Individual growth, well-being, and satisfaction. This third measure focuses on the individual and has much to do with time involved versus benefits gained. In extended team projects, there usually is a growth in skills and group relationships.

> A critical question is, "Do members feel that their personal time was well spent during the group?"

The time aspect led me to add the word "satisfaction" to the two previous terms. One factor that causes individuals to hesitate to agree to work on group projects that are not required as part of their work assignment is unequal workload. Satisfaction, as I'm using it, has to do with satisfaction with workload—how much the individual did in relationship to what others did and whether that level of participation was perceived as fair or reasonable. Thus, members of the strategic planning group may vary in the way in which they perceived individual growth, well-being, and individual satisfaction as an outcome of this work group.

We can all probably think of situations in which we did more than our fair share of the work in a project. Perhaps we've also done less than our fair share at times. Variation in individual member participation levels from group to group is typical: some groups interest us more than others, some are more relevant to our particular talents, we may have more time to spare during one project as compared to another. Ideally, a member will mention at the beginning of a group any limitations to participation that exist.

Facilitators can play a part in reducing member dissatisfaction with member workload by encouraging discussions of workload at the beginning of projects in which work outside the group session is an issue. Dissatisfaction with workload is an important issue in collaborative groups.

Nature of Collaboration

Gray and Wood (1991) offer the following definition of collaboration:

> Collaboration occurs when a group of autonomous stakeholders of a problem domain engage in an interactive process, using shared rules, norms, and structures, to act or decide on issues related to that domain (p. 146).

Four elements essential to collaboration identified by Stallworth (1998) have relevance for facilitated groups:

- shared goal
- interdependence
- equal input
- shared decision making

Both leader and members would balance the relational needs of collaboration members with the task demands of the group. As a result, the resources, skills, knowledge, and perspectives brought by members would benefit the collaboration's ability to produce innovative and effective outcomes (Keyton & Stallworth, 2003, p. 243).

Leaders and facilitators have a similar desire to balance task and relationship. The extent to which collaborative effort is a factor in facilitation depends on context and the reason for the group's existence. Groups that meet for one time or during a series of meetings that take place very close in time may not view themselves as collaborative units but more as groups that have very specific goals. In such cases, the facilitator's task is to engender enough collaborative spirit to get the job done. If the reason for the meeting is important to the members, the group may have quite a high level of enthusiasm. Other groups have a broader purpose, meet regularly over a period of time, and view themselves as a cohesive group or team. Long-term groups, however, may experience a loss of commitment as barriers and frustrations occur (Katz, 1988).

Barriers to collaborative effort described by project team members working on collaborative leadership projects and reported by Kolb and Gray (2007) are of value to a discussion of facilitation. These barriers are listed in declining order of importance based on the number of teams that mentioned each barrier. Other factors mentioned were dysfunctional alliances, lack of collaborative skills, logistics, frustration with the process, and individual agendas.

Exhibit 2-2
Top Barriers to Collaborative Effort

1. Missing or unclear goal
2. Individuals not pulling individual weight on the project
3. Lack of time
4. Lack of resources

Source: Kolb, J. A., & Gray, B. L. (2007). Using collaborative alliances to build leadership capacity: A five-year initiative. *Central Business Review, 26*(1), 11–16.

Goals, time, and resources have been previously discussed as inputs that affect group process and are consistently identified in the literature as important factors for group work. In the above section on group output, individual satisfaction was added to the third criteria measuring output and was described as it related to workload issues. This imbalance in workload has been described as **free riding,** defined as "a group member who receives benefits from group membership but who does not bear a fair share of the costs of producing these benefits" (Albanese et al., 1997, p. 512). Such members may also be labeled "cheap riders" (Stigler, 1974), and the concept has also been referred to as **social loafing** (Harkins & Jackson, 1985; Latane, Williams, & Harkins, 1979). We know that as additional people are added to a group, the tendency exists for some members to let others do the work. The amount of work that members are willing to expend on a group project is considered a primary factor in work group effectiveness (Hackman, 1990; Hirokawa & Keyton, 1995).

Advice to managers in dealing with free riders includes (1) keeping the group size as small as possible, (2) selecting members who are committed to the group's purpose, (3) selecting individuals who see the group's purpose as important to their careers, and (4) making the work of each group member identifiable (Albanese et al., 1997). In adapting this advice to facilitators, we see once again the importance of group size and member commitment and the importance and interlinked nature of inputs and group process. Excellent process can go only so far.

In work teams, poor performance by individual members has long been a problem (Kolb, 1996a; Larson & LaFasto, 1989), but this issue is typically handled by the manager or leader of the group rather than by a facilitator. Poor individual performance becomes relevant to the work of facilitators when we meet with groups over an extended period of time on a project that involves a substantial amount of work. If a leader is present in addition to a facilitator, which is generally the case in a work team, then work performance is the leader's responsibility. In groups that don't have a leader and/or in situations in which members themselves divide workload, the facilitator can play a role in seeing that workload issues are raised early on. Otherwise, the most organized and willing people will burn out as they increasingly take on more and more of group project loads. This imbalance in workload also, of course, affects relationships among group members and group climate. We now move on to a discussion of the two basic components of group work: task and relationship.

Task and Relationship Aspects of Groups

The dual needs of small groups were first recognized by Bales (1950) and Benne and Sheats (1948). These and other early scholars were consistent in the use of the "task" label; labels for the second dual need included socioemotional, mainte-nance, and relationship. The latter is the most commonly used term today. Schein (1979; 1987) applied this early work to process consultation. He described task or content as the work to be done by the group. Task process focuses on ways of get-ting the job done. This includes such things as setting an agenda, the use of decision-making and/or problem-solving techniques, and time management. Maintenance process is

31

described as ways of getting the group's psychosocial needs met and the development of satisfying relationships among group members. This includes such things as levels of participation, power issues, dealing with dysfunctional members, and setting appropriate norms of behavior.

Sixty years after this early work, task and maintenance functions are still recognized as central to group functioning. Reddy (1994) suggests the following questions be asked by the facilitator: "Is the group operating effectively? Is the group running efficiently? Are members satisfied with what they are doing and how they are doing it?" (p. 29).

You will read more about task and relationship/maintenance issues in the next chapter, in Chapters 6 and 7, and throughout the book. For now, just think about task as getting the job done and relationship as being able to work together well enough to accomplish the task. Some groups are very task oriented; others have a stronger focus on relationships among the members. An example of a task focus would be a business group working to reach a deadline on an important project. A group of people who meet regularly to discuss and help each other solve problems that arise in an area such as raising twins has more of a relationship focus.

In related work, Gouran and Hirokawa (2003) also emphasize the importance of helping members overcome the obstacles posed by **cognitive, affiliative,** and **egocentric** constraints.

Cognitive constraints involve feelings of pressure deriving from limited time or information. Affiliative constraints arise when concerns about maintaining relationships surpass those relating to successful task performance. Egocentric constraints are those involving dominance tendencies and other forms of self-serving interaction (p. 33).

Groups that work together over a period of time change and, ideally, grow in managing group task and relationships. Task and relationships are both part of a healthy functioning group. Individual group members may also exhibit egocentric or self-serving behaviors that serve their own needs—needs that are at odds with the needs of the group. These behaviors may be only a slight annoyance and cause some frustration and delay, or they may create a significant impediment to a group completing its task. As a group becomes a more cohesive unit, self-serving behaviors should diminish, although it is unrealistic to suggest that these behaviors disappear. If your work as a facilitator involves mostly working with a variety of short-term groups, you will experience first hand the effect of all three constraints.

Summary

In this chapter, I discussed open systems theory as it applies to groups, components of group inputs and outputs, the nature of collaboration and barriers to that effort, and task and relationship aspects of groups. I next move specifically to facilitation and discuss a framework for facilitation that is used throughout Part Two. This framework builds upon the dual needs of task and relationship as discussed in this chapter and includes elements that are critical for the process management nature of facilitation.

References

Albanese, R., Franklin, G. M., & Wright, P. (1997). *Management* (rev. ed.). Houston, TX: Dame Publications.

Bales, R. F. (1950). *Interaction profile analysis: A method for the study of small groups.* New York: Free Press.

Benne, K. D., & Sheats, P. (1948). Functional roles of group members. *Journal of Social Issues, 4*, 41–49.

Gouran, D. S., & Hirokawa, R. Y. (2003). Effective decision making and problem solving in groups: A functional perspective. In R. Y. Hirokawa, R. S. Cathcart, L. A. Samovar, & L. D. Henman (Eds.). *Small group communication: Theory and practice* (8th ed.; pp. 27–38). Los Angeles, CA: Roxbury.

Gray, B., & Wood, D. J. (1991). Collaborative alliances: Moving from practice to theory. *Journal of Applied Behavioral Science, 27*, 3–22.

Hackman, J. R. (1990). Introduction. Work teams in organizations: An orienting framework. In J. R. Hackman (Ed.), *Groups that work (and those that don't)* (pp. 1–14). San Francisco: CA: Jossey-Bass.

Harkins, S. G., & Jackson, J. M. (1985). The role of evaluation in eliminating social loafing. *Personality and Social Psychology Bulletin, 11*, 457–465.

Hirokawa, R. Y., & Keyton, J. (1995). Perceived facilitators and inhibitors of effectiveness in organizational work teams. *Management Communication Quarterly, 8*, 424–446.

Katz, R. (1988). High performance research teams. In R. Katz (Ed.). *Managing professionals in innovative organizations: A collection of readings* (pp. 315–331), Cambridge, MA: Ballinger Publishing.

Keyton, J., & Stallworth, V. (2003). On the verge of collaboration: Interaction processes versus group outcomes. In L. R. Frey (Ed.), *Group communication in context* (2nd ed; pp. 235–262). Mahwah, NJ: Lawrence Erlbaum Associates.

Kolb, J. A. (1996a). A comparison of leadership behaviors and competencies in high- and average-performance teams. *Communication Reports, 9*, 173–183.

Kolb, J. A. (1996b). Let's bring structure back. *Management Communication Quarterly, 9*, 452–465.

Kolb, J. A., & Sandmeyer, L. E. (2008). Supporting project teams: A framework used in a university/community collaborative initiative. *Performance Improvement Quarterly, 21*(1), 61–76.

Kolb, J. A., & Gray, B. L. (2007). Using collaborative alliances to build leadership capacity: A five-year initiative. *Central Business Review, 26*(1), 11–16.

Larson, C. E., & LaFasto, F. M. J. (1989). *Teamwork: What must go right, what can go wrong.* Newbury Park, CA: Sage.

Latane, B., Williams, K., & Harkins, S. (1979). Many hands make light the work: The causes and consequences of social loafing. *Journal of Personality and Social Psychology, 37,* 822–832.

McCaskey, M. G. (1979). *A framework for analyzing work groups.* Harvard Business School Case 480–009. Boston, MA: Harvard Business School.

Reddy, W. (1994*). Intervention skills: Process consultation for small groups and teams.* San Diego, CA: Pfeiffer & Company.

Schein, E. H. (1979). Personal changes through interpersonal relationships. In W. Bennis, J. VanMaahen, E. H. Schein, & F. I. Steele (Eds.). *Essays in interpersonal dynamics.* Homewood, IL: Dorsey Press.

Schein, E. (1987). *Process consultation: vol. II: Lessons for managers and consultants.* Reading, MA: Addison-Wesley.

Schermerhorn, J. R. Jr. (1984). *Management for productivity.* New York: John Wiley & Sons.

Stallworth, V. (1998). *Building a model of interorganizational nonprofit collaboration.* Unpublished master's thesis. University of Memphis, TN.

Stigler, G. J. (1974). Free riders and collective action: An appendix to theories of economic regulation. *Bell Journal of Economics and Management Science, 5,* 359–365.

Part Two
Framework for
Facilitation

Description of the Framework for Facilitation

Key Concepts

- Development of framework
- Description and presentation of framework
- Suggestions for use

In the last chapter, I mentioned task and relationship needs and constraints. In this chapter, the dual roles of task and relationship appear again as two elements of the framework for facilitation. The development of the eight-element framework as well as the framework itself and suggestions for use are presented here. The framework is then used as a unifying theme for the remainder of the book.

Development of Framework

Bales in 1950 talked about maintaining an equilibrium or balance between the demands of group task and group relationship. The fact that task and relationship aspects of groups are still used 60 years later as the primary language to describe group process is evidence of the accuracy with which these dimensions identify crucial group issues. All groups have task and relationship components and issues. The balance of these components depends on the purpose of the group. Some groups are heavily task focused; in others, relationships developed among members are of primary importance.

Model of facilitator competencies. My colleagues and I (Kolb, Jin, & Song, 2008) used task and relationship as a starting point in developing a Model of Core Facilitator Competencies relevant for small group facilitators. For our research, we analyzed data from three different groups of experienced facilitators, a total of 108 individuals, to create a model that was grounded in, and expanded upon, the task and relationship dyad that has long been used to describe basic components of group work. The resultant model consists of the three clusters of task, relationship/climate, and communication. The expansion of relationship to relationship/climate and the addition of communication reflect our findings related to the importance of developing a supportive climate and the centrality of communication to the role of facilitation. An interdependent and reciprocal relationship exists among the three clusters; each one affects the others. The three clusters work holistically to influence group process. The overall model consists of the following five components:

- communication
- task
- relationship/climate
- organization
- professional ethics

The fourth component labeled organization supports communication, task, and relationship/climate. Professional ethics permeates the role of facilitator and affects many decisions made by people in this role.

Competencies are defined as "characteristics of people doing a certain kind of work" (Rothwell & Sullivan, 2005, p. 136). The term "competencies" is a bit broader than the term "KSA" (knowledge, skills, and abilities) and encompasses "knowledge, skills, aspects of self-image, social motives, traits, thought patterns, mind-sets, and ways of thinking, feeling, and acting" (Dubois & Rothwell, 2004, p. 16).

Components of collaborative leadership identified by Kolb and Gray (2007) were used along with the Kolb, Jin, and Song (2008) model to develop the framework for facilitation presented in this book. These components were originally developed for project teams working in the second phase, the last three years, of a five-year project. Collaborative leadership components were based on our experiences in working with teams during the first phase of the same project, information collected from members of those teams, an examination of related literature (Hackman, 1990; Heath & Sias, 1999; Larson & LaFasto, 1989; Gray, 1989; Kolb, 1996; Lipman-Blumen, 2000), and our collective experiences in working with a large number of teams over a period of years. As already mentioned, collaborative effort is important in many of the groups that commonly work with facilitators. Most specifically, groups that depend on voluntary contributions from members who are also performing other work duties need to find a way to keep those members committed and engaged throughout a project. The components of collaborative leadership from this project are listed below:

- common mission
- collective responsibility
- necessary resources and information
- respectful and supportive climate
- awareness of group process
- creativity
- capacity to deal with conflict

You will notice that issues similar to those covered in Chapter 2 are included. Groups need a clear goal or mission; they work best within a climate that respects individuals and supports group process; and they require information and resources. Members benefit from an understanding of process and a capacity to deal with conflict. Groups that harness creativity have a better chance of synergy resulting from their collective efforts.

Presentation and Description of Framework

Facilitators pull all this together and help groups manage task and relationship/climate issues. The following Framework for Facilitation presented in Figure 3-1 combines the elements that I believe are most relevant for the type of facilitation described in this book. Communication, task, and relationships and climate form the center of the circle. The elements of organization and planning, values and ethics, conflict, creativity, and techniques appear in the outer circle.

Figure 3-1. Framework for Facilitation

Suggestions for Use

Each of the research-based elements of the Framework for Facilitation is discussed in the chapters that follow starting with Chapter 4, Organization and Planning. Chapter 4 draws together pertinent issues reviewed in the first two chapters of the book into a series of questions that can be used by the facilitator in organizing and planning facilitated groups. Chapter 5 moves into the inner cycle and discusses communication; Chapter 6, task; and Chapter 7, relationships and climate. As we move clockwise around the outer circle, values and ethics are found in Chapter 8, putting this discussion in the middle of the remaining chapters and allowing the reader to have a context for the issues raised. Chapter 9 covers conflict, Chapter 10, creativity, and Chapter 11, techniques.

Each element is covered separately and is also linked to others throughout the book. You certainly need to have an understanding of relationships and climate before you can hope to handle conflict. Choosing and using an appropriate technique requires knowledge and understanding of all the other chapters, which is why techniques appear at the end of the book. All aspects of the framework come together to provide information that will help a facilitator work effectively with groups.

The elements that comprise the Framework for Facilitation have been expanded from the model of competencies. You may notice that Organization is now Organization and Planning, which reflects the importance of the work done prior to facilitation. Professional Ethics has become Values and Ethics: facilitator reflections on personal views of what is important in group work and how a facilitator most effectively works with members are included here. Communication, Task, and Relationships and Climate remain as is, which is no surprise given the centrality of communication role and the enduring importance of both task and relationship. Three additional elements—Conflict, Creativity, and Techniques—have been added from the collaborative leadership research. Techniques is an interpretation of the component, "awareness of group process." The expanded treatment of techniques in Part Three of this book stems from my belief that a knowledge and understanding of a variety of techniques is beneficial for facilitation. In my own facilitation work, I have gathered together and used techniques from several sources and disciplines. These techniques are described in Chapters 12 through 14.

Facilitator competencies. The Model of Core Facilitator Competencies described earlier was based on information collected from experienced practicing facilitators and resulted also in a list of 23 competencies. A self-rating version of these competencies is found in Appendix A. If you currently facilitate groups, you might want to complete this self-assessment before you read the remainder of the book and then reassess when you finish after you've had a chance to think about the various aspects of facilitation. If you are just getting started in facilitation, I suggest you complete the assessment after you read the book.

In the section below, I have placed these competencies in italics under the appropriate chapter headings. These competencies are included in chapter discussions along with other related research, practical suggestions, and experiences and examples from my own work with groups.

Chapter 4, Organization and Planning:

Demonstrates evidence of advance planning and preparation
Completes appropriate follow-up activities as contracted

Chapter 5, Communication:

Listens actively
Paraphrases and summarizes segments of content
Clarifies perspectives in disagreements
Uses questions skillfully
Uses body language and nonverbals effectively
Observes and attends to nonverbals in group

Chapter 6, Task:

Keeps group focused on issues
Helps groups clarify purpose and establish ground rules
Uses techniques appropriate for task and group (expanded in Chapter 11)
Remains neutral as to task outcome (expanded in Chapter 8)
Adheres to established time frames
Uses appropriate technology and visual aids

Chapter 7, Relationships and Climate:

Creates a climate that supports interaction and discussion
Encourages group involvement in and ownership of issues/task
Uses humor effectively
Monitors group dynamics
Maintains adherence to ground rules
Provides feedback and encourages process skills
Handles disruptive individual(s) whose behavior is detrimental to the group

Chapter 8, Values and Ethics:

Remains neutral as to task outcome (repeat)

Chapter 9, Conflict:

Focuses group's attention on substantive issues in conflict

Chapter 10, Creativity:

Stimulates small group insights and creativity

Chapter 11, Techniques:

Uses techniques appropriate for task and group (repeat)

Descriptions of techniques are found in Part Three, Chapters 11 through 14.

Summary

In this chapter, I presented a Framework for Facilitation consisting of eight elements that are used as chapter headings in Part Two. As we move into Chapter 4, the focus is on asking questions and participating in advance planning that will help a facilitator assist a group in accomplishing its task and maintaining its relationships. Much of the success of a facilitated session depends on planning and setting realistic expectations that are agreed upon by all involved. The chapter also includes follow-up activities, a commonly neglected aspect of facilitation.

References

Bales, R. F. (1950). *Interaction profile analysis: A method for the study of small groups.* New York: Free Press.

Dubois, D. D., & Rothwell, W. J. (2004). *Competency-based human resource management.* Palo Alto, CA: Davies-Black Publishing.

Gray, B. (1989). Collaborating: *Finding common ground for multiparty problems.* San Francisco, CA: Jossey-Bass.

Hackman, J. R. (1990). *Groups that work (and those that don't).* San Francisco: Jossey-Bass.

Heath, R. G., & Sias, P. M. (1999). Communicating spirit in a collaborative alliance. *Journal of Applied Communication Research, 27,* 356–376.

Kolb, J. A. (1996). Let's bring structure back. *Management Communication Quarterly, 9,* 452–465.

Kolb, J. A., & Gray, B. L. (2007). Using collaborative alliances to build leadership capacity: A five-year initiative. *Central Business Review, 26*(2), 11–16.

Kolb, J. A., Jin, S., & Song, J. (2008). A model of small group facilitator competencies, *Performance Improvement Quarterly, 21*(2), 119-133.

Larson, C. E., & LaFasto, F. M. J. (1989). *Teamwork: What must go right, what can go wrong.* Newbury Park, CA: Sage.

Lipman-Blumen, J. (2000). *Connective leadership.* New York: Oxford University Press.

Rothwell, W. J., & Sullivan, R. L. (2005). Organization development. In W. J. Rothwell & R. L. Sullivan (Eds.), *Practicing organization development: A guide for consultants* (2nd ed; pp. 9–38). San Francisco, CA: Pfeiffer.

Organization and Planning

Key Concepts

- Asking preliminary questions
- Advance planning
- Logistics
- After the session

This chapter covers four aspects of organization and planning: asking preliminary questions; pre-planning the session including the agenda and other materials that are distributed prior and/or provided at site; taking care of logistics such as room and space arrangements, materials, and supplies; and planning what happens after the session. The longer I am involved in facilitation, the more I am convinced that much of the success of a group session is determined by what happens, or doesn't happen, before the session starts. You also need to keep the end in sight—not only what needs to be accomplished by the end of the session but what is expected to happen afterward as a result.

Small group facilitating usually, but not always, includes an initial background meeting prior to a face-to-face session with group members. I assume in this chapter that this process is followed, and that you have time for advance planning. If time is limited, revert to basic journalism questions and ask who, what, when, where, why, and how questions.

Asking Preliminary Questions

You have received a message requesting your services as a facilitator. Depending on the circumstances, you either may be expected to be there if the time works for your schedule (for example, if you work as a facilitator for one company or client) or you may have a choice about your participation and are being asked to consider accepting this job. In any event, there are questions you should ask in order to make decisions about how best to proceed.

One of the first statements uttered by a person asking you to facilitate a group might be some version of "this will be a fairly straightforward session." And it might be. But the process of asking preliminary questions could uncover relevant issues that have been forgotten or overlooked. Many of these questions relate to issues first raised in Chapter 2. Eight essential questions are covered in Exhibit 4-1.

Exhibit 4-1. Essential Questions

1. Is there a set date, time, and number of people?
2. What is the history, purpose, and expected outcome?
3. What is my role?
4. Do I need to revisit question 1?
5. To what extent were group leaders and/or members involved in the decision to invite me to facilitate their session?
6. What technology is available?
7. Am I willing to move forward?
8. Have we come to an agreement?

Each of these questions is discussed in order. As we cover these, you may think of additional questions that you have used in the past.

Is there a set date, time, and number of people? Basically, you need to know how much of the session has already been planned and how much leeway you have. This is important not only for your schedule but also in terms of the time you have for advance preparation and the fundamental issue of whether what is planned suits the time frame. Many meetings are destined to fail because there simply is not time to accomplish the set agenda. You will need to revisit this issue after you receive additional information.

What is the history, purpose, and expected outcome? You want to probe for as much detail as possible here. Ask questions about prior sessions with this group on related topics. If you are coming in to facilitate a follow-up session or to help the group reach another milestone on an exiting project, any information you can get on what happened before will be useful. What were the outcomes? How is this session different? Are the participants willing to continue with these sessions, or are they becoming frustrated? Is there a history of discord on the issues to be covered? What is the relationship among the expected participants (coworkers, a mixture of titles and hierarchy levels within an organization, people who don't know each other at all)? Have members seen and/or agreed to an agenda?

What is my role? Remember Chapter 1. Are you being asked to be a pure process facilitator or to fulfill a dual role such as leader/facilitator, facilitator/content matter expert, facilitator/ trainer, facilitator/mediator, or perhaps some other combination? What are the expectations for your participation prior to the meeting and after the meeting? A session may end with sheets covered with issues and options generated by the group. Are you responsible for capturing this information and in what format? Is there a designated group leader? If you are an external person, is there an internal facilitator who will also be present? Are you going to be working with someone to prepare an agenda? Are there any ethical issues that might compromise your role—your inability to be neutral or to serve in a dual role? Perhaps something has come up in the discussion that causes you some concerns—if so, mention it now. Listen to any misgivings you have. Although it is possible to overdo asking questions, facilitators generally suffer from too little, rather than too much, information.

Do I need to revisit Question 1? Question 1: Is there a set date, time, and number of people? Does the composition of the groups and the number seem appropriate? Now that you have additional information, do you believe that the designated time is sufficient to accomplish the desired purpose? If not, raise this issue now. Perhaps you have misjudged the situation, but voice your concerns. Ask to contact other people if you believe this is necessary.

To what extent were group leaders and/or members involved in the decision to invite you to facilitate their session? If members did not have any input into the decision, this may or may not be important, depending on the nature of the situation and the group. People in charge of planning meetings commonly contact colleagues to receive names of experienced facilitators. If you are an internal facilitator, your name most likely appears on a list or a web page. At times, group members are asked to submit names of facilitators to the person planning the meeting. Once it has been determined that you will facilitate this session, a desirable next step is to establish contact with group members as described in the next section.

What technology is available? What types of group technology systems are available? Are members familiar with such systems? Have they used them previously? What types of electronic communication systems are in place that may be used by the facilitator prior to the session? Is anyone planning to participate from a distance? If so, become familiar with the technology that is to be used and keep this in mind when planning the meeting. Also decide what materials should be posted or distributed to all participants prior to the meeting and whether any preliminary decisions should be made before the face-to-face session. Consider how technology can be used before and after the meeting for notification and follow-up purposes.

Am I willing to move forward with this facilitation? Is my skill set appropriate for this assignment? Do I have sufficient time for whatever planning I believe is necessary? Did any bells go off that would cause me to reconsider accepting this facilitation? Did any ethical issues arise? Will I need a cofacilitator or someone to help with technology?

Have both parties come to an agreement? What is included in this agreement and the level of formality are determined by a variety of factors. I've found that putting things in writing helps clarify roles and expectations. You may decide that an e-mail suffices. The important thing is that discussions and decisions occur prior to the actual session. A sample memo of agreement appears in Appendix B.

Advance Planning

Plan based on the desired outcome of the scheduled session(s). Work backward from that to determine what needs to be done prior to the facilitation. I am assuming that this planning is for a face-to-face session although, of course, other options exist.

Discussions. As soon as possible, work with either an internal facilitator or someone familiar with group needs to develop a plan for the session, including what materials will be distributed ahead of time and what work, if any, members should be expected to complete before the session. Decisions require accurate information. Members may be able to provide this information at the session itself. Often, however, information needs to be collected and, perhaps, distributed prior to the scheduled session. For example, prior to a decision of a site selection for a conference, each of the members might be responsible for collecting detailed information pertaining to one site—hotel costs, travel options, conference facilities, and so on. Someone other than the facilitator is probably in charge of these content details. Your job is to ensure that members are clear about the information expected and the timeline. Content matter experts might be invited for a portion of the meeting. You might make the decision that two sessions are necessary: one to decide on criteria for decision making and a second, after a period of data collection, to make the actual choice.

Preparing the agenda and related information. The most basic purpose of an agenda is to provide a description and timeline for the session: what is happening when. This is distributed ahead of time, how far ahead depends in part on how much preparation time is needed by participants. People are requested to respond if they have additional information that should be included or any feedback on the plan for the session. If some members are to be arriving late or leaving early, you need to decide on a core time when all will be present. In a crucial meeting, ideally all essential participants will be present for the full meeting. However, it may be that some individuals are scheduled to come in to give background information or to be available for questions but are not expected to take part in the actual decision making. It is becoming more common for participants to agree ahead of time to limit use of electronic devices during the meeting. People limit checking e-mail to the breaks and leave the meeting to take phone calls only if those calls are urgent. Agreements depend on norms of the people involved, the type of industry, and the urgency of the meeting. Regardless of what has been decided, if something unusual happens right before the meeting, all agreements are off, and you simply do the best you can.

At one meeting I facilitated, participants learned the day before the half-day session that an important top executive would unexpectedly be coming to town in two days. Since scheduling this meeting had been quite difficult, we agreed to go ahead. Before we started, we talked about how this news would affect the day's session. We decided to have two breaks to allow people to check e-mails and make important calls; everyone agreed to try to be focused on the task during the meeting. Some people moved to the back of the room to work on reports, and we called on them when their expertise was needed. Actually, the session was very productive. The special circumstances worked in our favor, I believe. Participants wanted to use their time well and they did.

Agenda format. There are differences of opinion on the level of detail that is preferable for an agenda. Agendas for retreats and other half-day or full-day sessions generally provide an overall schedule of the session events and indicate specific times for opening activities, breaks, and meal times. This gives people advance knowledge of times when they can return calls or check messages and also is necessary for making arrangements for food and beverages. In routine shorter meetings, practices vary. The agenda should include the name of the group, date and time of the meeting, a listing of items to be covered, and other detail as desired.

Preferences for the order of agenda items also vary. Some facilitators prefer to discuss difficult items right after one or two brief opening agenda items in order to ensure that sufficient time is allowed and to give people a sense of accomplishment. Another approach is to include all brief and noncontroversial items first and save the items requiring the most time and discussion for the end. The approach you select depends on your assessment of what is best for each group. If you choose to have the most important item near the end, make sure that you save three minutes for wrap up. An important discussion that runs right to the end of the meeting time with no closure is frustrating.

Another choice is how much structure to include: some very structured agendas included a time allotment for each agenda item and a declaration of whether it involves announcement of information (I), a discussion (D), or an action item such as a vote (A). Others simply list the activities in order and do not specify a timeline. The first has the advantage of clarity, but the disadvantage of limiting options based on what occurs during the session. The latter may lead to excessive time being spent on items that are unimportant and a resultant lack of time for important discussion items. Be sure that the agenda items are stated clearly. If group members might be surprised by an item, provide a rationale. Seibold and Krikorian (1997) give the following example of an agenda item for a finance committee:

Item 3. To formalize our policy on request for services from persons uninsured and unable to pay.

Reasons: There has been a 6% increase in these cases since last year and the Board of Directors has requested by April 1 an analysis by the Finance Committee of the cost of these cases for the Operations Budget. (p. 282)

If people are going to be coming in and going out during the session, having a running timeline for the session is necessary in order to ensure that individuals know when voting will occur and when items in which they have the most interest will be discussed. Groups within organizations tend to have norms that relate to the amount of structure and detail that is customary, so be sure to check that and follow standard procedure unless there is a reason to do something in a different way.

If you do manage to accomplish all items on the agenda, you will be doing better than most groups. In results reported in 1995 on meetings observed in 35 organizations, 17 percent of groups never got to all the items on the agenda (Volkema & Neiderman, 1995). In this same study, although 66 percent used both an agenda and documents during meetings, only 26 percent distributed both before the meetings. These study results give some indication of why people become frustrated with meetings and why facilitators are in demand.

Including information on the facilitator. Include a brief paragraph about you and your background. If you are asking members to respond to the agenda, this summary, sometimes called a biosketch, can be distributed then. Or perhaps this information was distributed at the time you were selected. The important thing is that members should be given some pertinent information about you prior to the day of the session. You don't want to open the session talking about yourself. In the biosketch, stress the information that is most relevant for this group. An example for someone serving as a facilitator/content matter expert at a teacher inservice meeting follows:

Janice Martin taught 10th grade in the Houston public schools for seven years before returning to school to receive a master's degree in social psychology. She has ten years' experience as a small group facilitator. Her specialty is helping groups work better collaboratively and, in particular, finding approaches to handle dysfunctional behavior in groups, which is the topic of our inservice today.

Other information. The basic rule is "no surprises." If participants are to dress casually or bring something special or if they have agreed to certain things, list this information on materials sent in advance. Note: ask about norms of attire so that you will dress with the appropriate level of formality or informality. I can remember being told "please don't wear a suit." This turned out to be good advice. Everyone at the session was casually dressed; I wore khakis, a cotton top, and a casual blazer, which was perhaps one step dressier than the participants. This seemed exactly right, and I could have removed the blazer if I felt overdressed. How you are dressed sends a message and helps create a climate.

Logistics

The room and space. Where is the session being held? How large is the room ? Are there movable tables or desks? Is the room wired for technology? What are the arrangements for breaks and meals? Go to the site and look at the room if at all possible. Does the room have windows? Do the windows open? Is any noisy work scheduled close to this location? The temperature of the room could be an issue. Too hot, too cold, rarely does everyone agree. The rule is that too cold is preferable to too hot. If you haven't personally experienced conference room temperatures, notice the number of veteran conference attendees who show up with heavy sweaters on even the hottest summer day.

Logistics are important. The most complaints I ever received at a session was because of a last-minute change in location from a fairly large conference room in a hotel to a small meeting room that was part of an association's suite of offices. I managed to move us to a larger space, but some of the participants remained irritated at the session planners for changing the initial location. We did accomplish the purpose of the session and managed to have a fairly pleasant experience, but the beginning of the day was frustrating for all involved. At another meeting, the people setting up lunch began about 30 minutes early and were so noisy that I had to ask them to stop. This interruption, of course, caused everyone to focus on lunch, so I needed to quickly wrap up what we were doing. Luckily, this lost time was not a problem, and I made sure that subsequent meetings in this hotel were arranged differently with lunch in a separate room. The point to remember is assume that some things might go wrong and be sure to have phone numbers (and specific names of people) to call if problems occur with room arrangement, heating, plumbing, or refreshments.

Table placement. There are several options for placement of tables and desks. In a large group of 40 or more, having people sit at round tables placed close to each other but with enough room for the facilitator and participants to walk between them works well. In this manner, people can work in small groups and also be close enough to discuss as a large group. Two flip chart easels should be placed at the front of the room for the use of the facilitator with additional flip charts available for small group use.

An alternate arrangement for medium- to large-sized groups is to place rectangular tables seating two to four people in two rows with the facilitator in the front. This generally works well if the facilitator plans to be standing during much of the meeting and/or if the facilitator will be working as a facilitator/trainer or facilitator/content matter expert. If the group and the facilitator will be seated for the majority of the time, two conference tables pushed together to form a large square is a way for people to see each other and the facilitator. The conference table arrangement is best for groups of 15 or less and gives people space for documents. A large round table can also be used. A U-shaped arrangement of tables with the facilitator again at the front is another choice that gives flexibility. The facilitator can stand in the open section of the U and have access to all members. Members can see each other but, if the table is long, people seated next to each other might begin pockets of conversation that can be distracting.

Techniques, materials, and supplies. Later on in this book, I cover a variety of techniques that can be used for decision making, problem solving, and strategic planning. Each of you reading this probably has techniques that you like to use. Several of these techniques require specific equipment and materials such as flip charts, markers, index cards, to mention only a few. I always run through the entire procedure in my mind to be sure that I have everything I need. I also have a kit of items that I always take to facilitated sessions, just in case I need them (see Exhibit 4-2).

Exhibit 4-2. Tool Kit

✓ Flip chart paper
✓ Markers
✓ Stick-on pads for individuals to record and post ideas
✓ Index cards for giving feedback or organizing ideas
✓ Tape
✓ Stick-on dots for voting
✓ Sheets of plain 8½" x 11" paper for list making
✓ Name tents
✓ Pens

My view is that you plan the session and the materials you will need ahead of time, but you also are flexible and able to move in a different direction as the situation warrants. I can think of several occasions in which I have had people write a thought or feedback on an index card or piece of paper and put it in the middle of the table prior to break. This can be a response to a question, a vote, or simply feedback to the session thus far. Bringing materials allows you a myriad of options.

Also, I always request from the site at least one easel with flip chart paper that I use to write the name of the session. I prefer to have two easels with paper since that can speed up the idea-recording phase of many techniques. In one case when I was facilitating with another person, there was some confusion about the order in which we were to do certain things. When one discussion was moved, some handouts we had prepared with process questions were no longer relevant. We called a brief break and wrote new discussion questions on flip chart paper. The participants did not ever realize that we made a change and the new questions led us directly where we needed to go. Again, having materials available extends your options. From the participants' viewpoint, everything should run seamlessly. Unless your purpose is to teach process, the techniques and tools you use should be transparent, not really noticed on their own but effective to accomplish the purpose of the session.

Once you have collected information that allows you to plan a session, give thought to what procedures and techniques you might use. Think about the advantages and disadvantages of each, and consult with members if you have any doubts about suitability of a specific approach. This is covered in greater detail in Chapter 6 and in Part Three.

After the Session

If you are using materials such as flip charts, you may finish the session with several flip charts filled with suggestions, decisions, and questions taped around the room. What happens to this material? If you are fortunate enough to have someone helping, that person can bring a computer and enter data from the sheets as they are completed. These materials can be sent to participants via e-mail, posted on a web site, or simply copied and distributed. Sessions often end with a Next Steps? question. What is your responsibility as a facilitator for what comes after the planned session? This, of course, depends in large part on agreements made earlier in the process.

As you plan the session, keep in mind what materials will be generated by whatever technique or procedure you choose and be certain to allow for what happens to participant output. If nothing has been decided, you might very well find yourself the custodian of these sheets. Now what? Managing output, especially during a day-long meeting, is one important aspect of choosing techniques that should receive careful consideration. Even if a clear decision has been reached, the information provided and questions recorded during the discussion are items that might be wanted. Confidentiality, of course, enters into this. Perhaps written materials should be discarded. The takeaway point is: what is to be saved, in what manner, and by whom. Does everyone agree on what should happen to materials generated during the meeting?

Summary

In this chapter, I have described the important first steps in planning a facilitated session. Asking relevant questions will help you decide on a plan of approach and will determine what, if anything, needs to be done by the participants prior to the facilitated session. You should verify that in advance of the day(s) of the meeting, members have received an agenda, know that you are going to facilitate, and have had an opportunity to provide input and/or ask questions. These advance planning steps are quite common and expected. What may be overlooked is a determination of the facilitator's responsibility for the input and materials generated during the meeting. Be sure that you know ahead of time what expectations are held for this final step and consider this in your planning. As we move to the next chapter, think about the importance of communication. Anyone who works as a facilitator is constantly communicating, either verbally, nonverbally, or both.

Chapter 5 focuses on communication.

References

Seibold, D. R., & Krikorian, D. H. (1997). Planning and facilitating group meetings. In L. W. Frey & J. K. Barge (Eds.), *Managing group life: Communicating in decision-making groups.* Boston: Houghton Miffln.

Volkema, R. J., & Niederman, F. (1995). Organizational meetings: Formats and information requirements. *Small Group Research, 26,* 3–24.

Communication

Key Concepts

- Meaning ≠ Meaning
- Listening, paraphrasing, and summarizing
- Clarifying issues and perspectives
- Asking questions
- Using and observing nonverbal communication

Everything we do sends a message. We cannot not communicate. Although it is certainly possible to overdo looking for messages, especially in the area of nonverbal communication, facilitators should be mindful of the effect of their communication behaviors and notice the behaviors of people in their groups. Communication affects all aspects of group facilitation. In this chapter, I focus on listening and clarifying meaning, asking questions that serve a purpose in group functioning, and understanding the power of nonverbal communication.

Transfer of Meaning

I'll start with one of my favorite sayings: meaning does not equal meaning.

Meaning ≠ Meaning

Whenever I use this phrase, people respond with head nods and stories about how meaning varies among people. This is especially relevant for group communication since so many people are involved. It is naïve to assume that everyone understands everyone else.

In any dialogue, what I understood that you said may or may not be what you intended to say. There are many reasons for this. If you say, "Please bring home a gallon of milk," to a longstanding partner or roommate, this request needs little clarification. The listener knows what kind of milk (full, 2%, 1%, non-fat, organic), what brand, and what type of packaging. If someone is staying with you for a brief time and has volunteered to run errands, milk on a list, without clarification, may result in the person bringing home what she or he usually buys. Not a disaster, of course. But the recipient of the message has made an assumption about meaning that may or may not be correct. In today's world, the visitor might very well call from the market and ask "What kind of milk?" Often, however, the recipient of a message is not even aware that a misinterpretation may have occurred.

Imagine the levels of misunderstanding that might occur with more important and involved messages. A person new to a business group, for example, does not have the context or awareness of group norms that exist in long-term members. Think for a moment about how much we assume the person already understands. Remember your first days and weeks at a new job and all the questions you asked. As we get to know people, we assume more and explain less. This is natural behavior and saves time. If you ask me to make 10 copies for a meeting and I say, "If I understand you correctly, you want me to make 10 copies on standard 8½" x 11" paper," you will be more than a bit irritated and probably think I'm dense. There is no need to clarify every message. However, missed deadlines, hurt feelings, and quite serious conflicts may occur because of simple misunderstanding of meaning. Once we know people, we assume that we know what the person means. Only when something goes wrong do we realize we should have asked questions.

The above examples assume that the person in each case heard what was said but failed to understand. But how often do we not even hear something important because we weren't really listening. Most of us, if we're honest with ourselves, will admit that we could improve our listening skills.

Active Listening

Active listening is important for yourself and for group members. So, what does this mean? Although this phrase is sometimes used to refer to the ability to repeat information that is given you—i.e., paraphrasing—my preferred definition as related to group work is the following:

> **active listening**: being in the moment, paying close attention to the points the person is making and asking yourself if you understand or if you need to ask questions

Consider the difference between hearing and listening. Most of us become very skilled throughout the years at giving the impression we are listening. We can look at the speaker, nod our heads, and pay partial attention while our minds are occupied in thinking through a personal issue or planning the rest of our day. This might be called lazy listening or benign neglect. We aren't making any judgments that cause us to ignore the speaker; we simply are choosing to focus on other matters.

Perhaps we've acquired some annoying habits such as doing other things while someone is speaking or assuming we know what the person is going to say without giving him or her the chance to say it. We may, if we're polite, refrain from interrupting, but we already know what our response will be and wish the person would hurry up and make his point. We're not listening; we're waiting to speak. If you're not sure how closely you listen, try an experiment. Assume that you are going to be asked to repeat what a person just said to you to someone else. Give your full attention to the speaker. How difficult is this for you? If you find it exhausting, this will give you some idea of your usual listening habits.

As a facilitator, you need to be aware of your own listening behaviors as well as those of people in the group. Go through the following list of irritating listening behaviors, check the ones that you find annoying, and circle the ones that apply to yourself.

Exhibit 5-1. Irritating Listening Habits

❑ 1. He is always rushing ahead of my story and guessing my point—he sometimes even finishes my sentences for me.

❑ 2. She interrupts me when I am talking.

❑ 3. He never looks at me when I talk. I don't know if he is listening or not.

❑ 4. She continually fidgets with a pencil, cleans her glasses, looks at her watch, or does something else while I am talking.

❑ 5. He overdoes being attentive—too many head nods, or "mm-mms" or "uh-huhs." I feel like he really isn't listening.

❑ 6. She never smiles—I'm afraid to talk to her.

❑ 7. He asks questions as if he doubts everything I say.

❑ 8. Whenever I make a suggestion, she throws cold water on it.

❑ 9. He asks questions that demand agreement with his ideas; for example, he makes a statement and then says, "Don't you think so?" or "Don't you agree?"

❑ 10. She frequently answers a question with another question—usually it's one I can't answer. It embarrasses me.

❑ 11. He reacts to one word or idea—I don't have a chance to finish stating my case.

❑ 12. Everything I say reminds her of an experience she has had or an idea or story she's heard. I get frustrated when she continually interrupts to say, "That reminds me..."

❑ 13. When I have a good idea, he takes credit for it by saying something like, "Oh, yes, I have been thinking about that, too."

continued

(continued)

> ❏ 14. She stares at me when I'm talking and looks me in the eye so directly that I feel self-conscious.
>
> ❏ 15. He inserts humorous remarks when I am trying to be serious.

If you are like most of us, you will see yourself in several of these statements. Perhaps you can add other irritating habits. This gives you a good idea of what to look for in your group member behaviors. Some facilitators include "Don't interrupt" as a norm of behavior or ground rule for the group.

I talked about norms of behavior in Chapter 2. Some norms of good listening include taking turns in speaking, allowing others to speak without interruption, avoiding side conversations or other distractions when someone is speaking, not assuming you know the person's point, and asking questions that indicate you were paying attention. Paraphrasing and summarizing are closely related to listening.

Paraphrasing and Summarizing

An important job of a facilitator is the ability to help people pay attention to group dialogue: in short, to help them become better listeners. This generally involves repeating what has been said and making sure that you and the group understand the meaning. You might find that individuals in the group have a variety of interpretations of what someone said, depending on their definitions of words, their response to trigger words, or simply careless listening. Note the following exchange:

> **Susan:** I think we need to begin working on our project presentation. Who has ideas?
>
> **Lee:** I think we need to be sure to cover all objections that others will have. Be sure we address concerns.

Jim: I don't agree. Why raise issues that people can use to criticize our ideas? Let's just go with the strengths.

Susan: I agree with Jim. We have a limited amount of time. Why focus on negatives?

Lee: I don't view addressing concerns as focusing on negatives.

Jim: We don't have time for that. Should this be a formal presentation?

Romina: I think it needs to be formal. We need handouts. Does everyone agree?

Heads nod—all agree. They start to talk about content.

If you were the facilitator, how would you paraphrase this conversation? They've all agreed that the presentation should be formal. They've agreed, somewhat, that they don't want the presentation to be negative. But is there agreement on what they mean by formal and not negative? Maybe, but most likely, no. A useful action or intervention at this point would be to state that there appears to be agreement that the presentation should be formal. Does everyone agree on what that means? What are some words that describe a formal presentation? Make a list of what people say and then be sure that everyone agrees on exactly what is meant by a formal presentation.

Before people begin working on content, you might restate the comments about "not negative" and ask Lee to expand on what he meant by "addressing concerns." Perhaps he could give an example. When asked, Lee might say:

I see this as being proactive. Let them realize that we have taken into consideration factors that might go against the success of the project. It is a stronger presentation if we mention these points rather than wait for others to raise them.

Then you, as facilitator, might ask if this fits in with "not negative." Whatever conversation follows or whatever decision is made, at least members understand each other's word choices and issues.

Words often serve as triggers or are used to mean a variety of things. Remember Chapter 1 and the multiple meanings of the word "facilitate." An important job of the facilitator is to make sure that people clarify terms and understand each other. Otherwise, you have one member or members spending an enormous amount of time on a "formal" presentation involving elaborate animated slides when others in the group intended only that the presentation be delivered standing using a well-designed handout instead of seated without any handout.

Although Lee's comments might not be viewed as rising to the level of disagreement, depending on what is said during the follow-up, you did clarify meaning. Disagreements may arise that are not over substance but instead over varying interpretations of words. The word "conflict," for example, causes dread in some people, although there is general agreement that conflict about issues is a positive group behavior.

Clarifying Issues and Perspectives in Disagreements

Your role as a facilitator is to ask sufficient questions to ensure that group members understand the issues involved in the disagreement and the viewpoints expressed by other people.

You might say, for example:

> Jennifer, you don't want to move into the Asian Pacific market.

> Alice, you do. Could you each state reasons for your belief?

With this restatement, you paraphrase and then move on to clarifying issues and areas of disagreement. Ask as many clarifying questions as are necessary to bring out all issues. Ask the group, "What questions do you have for Jennifer? For Alice? It is always a good idea to list these reasons for everyone to see. Your goal is to encourage questions that will clarify issues and also move people away from overly emotional discourse based on a "for or against" stance and toward a rational conversation of issues and concerns. You might then move on to points of agreement. Expand the discussion to include the opinions of the entire group. There are a variety of approaches that might be chosen to make a decision on what to do, but step one almost always involves making sure that all issues are explored and understood and that points of disagreement and reasons for varying opinions are clear. You want people to focus on issues rather than positions. "For" or "against" is a strong statement that essentially stops communication. Statements such as, "I feel strongly about this issue because..." move the conversation forward. A discussion of reasons for positions and issues involves a conversation that may, or may not, lead to an identification of an approach that satisfies all concerned. In our earlier example, an exploration of a move into Asian Pacific markets that involves only one product line might be a workable approach.

Much of what you do as a facilitator involves asking the group to slow down and make sure issues, comments, and points of view are understood. Another important competency of a facilitator is to use questions that accomplish both task and relationship goals.

Asking Questions

Questions are phrased in a variety of ways and used for multiple purposes. The role of a facilitator involves knowing what questions to ask and when and how to ask them.

Characteristics of questions. Questions can be classified as either limited or open ended. **Limited questions** ask for a brief, specific answer that generally gives information or expresses an opinion. Examples include:

Would you rather use a pen or a pencil?
What day is the report due?
Do you agree with John's idea?

Open-ended questions imply a wide range of possible answers and encourage elaboration. Examples of such questions are:

What do you like about this suggestion?
What are the pros and cons of this idea?
How do you suggest we proceed?

There is a place in group discussion for both types of questions. "Is this a good time for a break?" is a useful limited question. After a rather long discussion of an issue when questions and comments appear to have ceased, questions such as "Are all issues on the table?" or "Is there a need for further discussion?" seek agreement on whether there is closure on one segment of a discussion or process. These questions appear limited but, in fact, can be answered with greater detail if someone chooses to extend the discussion.

Types of questions. Brilhart (1986) describes three types of group process questions. I have changed the focus slightly to phrase these for facilitator use.

- *Orientation-seeking questions* bring members back from unrelated discussions or clarify the purpose of the session. Examples include: What are we trying to accomplish with this discussion? Is this discussion helpful right now or should we put it aside until later? Is our purpose to reach agreement on the best policy or to increase our understanding of the issue? and This question has raised a number of interesting questions. Should we make a list of those for later use and move back to the issue at hand?

- *Procedure-seeking questions* relate to a procedure or technique that is being suggested or in use or general questions about process that are unrelated to content.

69

Questions might combine information giving with a question such as:

We could have each person offer one suggestion at a time in round robin format as I write them on the board or you could each write your suggestions on index cards and then post them on the board. Which would you prefer?" or

This step in the procedure usually takes 30 minutes. Do you want a break now or after?

People might hesitate to ask questions if they think they might appear foolish, so explain procedures fully and encourage group members to ask questions as you move through a process. You might ask, "What are reasons for the rule that each person has three votes but cannot use them all to vote for one solution?" This allows you to remind people of the procedure while also explaining how three votes from one person for one solution would slant the outcome.

You may have a reason to have group members perform a procedure in a certain way. In that case, you would just explain the procedure and ask if there are any questions before you begin. Research by Hirokawa (1980) found that discussion of procedure is useful to a point. Everyone needs to understand procedures that will be followed. Too much discussion of procedure, however, is counterproductive and limits the time available for discussion and problem solving. Your goal is to have everyone understand the purpose and steps of a particular decision-making or problem-solving technique before you begin. A distribution of materials prior to the meeting might be useful in this regard. Providing linking statements between steps is a way to remind people what has already happened and what is upcoming. An example would be: Now that we've identified criteria, we are going to assign an importance number from 1–10 to each one. This can be a little confusing. Do you want to review this before we start?

- *Relational questions* refer to how members feel toward each other, toward the group, or toward the facilitator. In the beginning of the session when you explain your role, you might ask if anyone has any question about your function in the group. If you have a dual role such as leader/facilitator, you may want to ask if there is anything you could do that would help this dual role be more comfortable for the group. During a discussion of ground rules, invite questions about the rules. You could ask, for example, How would we phrase a comment when we don't agree with someone's idea? I find it useful to use humor and give extreme examples such as "That idea is even worse than the one you had two weeks ago," or "That suggestion makes no sense at all." There are some quick ways to make a point about how we should consider the feelings and respect the opinions of others even if we disagree with what they say. "I understand what you're saying, but I think we need to explore other options" is one example that allows points of disagreement to be raised.

  A final point under relational question is whether the facilitator uses the term "we" or "you" when referring to the group. For example, "have we reached a decision" versus "have you reached a decision." Each person needs to make this choice based on what seems appropriate and feels comfortable. I generally use "we" in questions related to process since, in my opinion, including myself in the group helps create a cohesive climate and indicates that I am an active participant. In questions of content, however, the use of "we" implies a level of facilitator knowledge and involvement that is contrary to fact. Examples would be, "Have you considered the impact of this decision on work schedules?" or "How much time do you have to implement the solution?" Using "we" suggests that the facilitator is affected by this decision or will be involved in the solution. If the facilitator will be continuing to work with the group on implementation, however, asking "How much time do we have?" would make sense.

Other examples. How the facilitator asks questions and communicates in general serves as a model for group members. Most facilitators have phrases that they find useful and that fit the way they communicate. The following list is not meant to be inclusive but gives an idea of the types of questions and comments that are commonly used by someone in the facilitator role:

- Have all important issues been raised? Is this list complete?

- The group seems frustrated to me. Is that a fair description? Why is that?

- Does anyone have any questions about the point/issue raised by Joon?

- Let's see if we can be specific about what is liked and not liked about this idea. What are the positives? Negatives?

- We seem to be at a good time to break. Do you agree? When we come back, we will...

- The points that have been raised are interesting and seem relevant. However, if we spend too much time on x, we won't get to y. Do you think it is necessary to spend time on *x?* If so, how long?

- Maria, please go on with your point. Would you explain what you mean?

- Do you all know what Joe means when he uses the term_____? Joe, would you please tell us how you're using this?

- Robert, you suggested___. How is this idea different from Peter's. Do we have the information we need to discuss each option?

- Have we separated fact from opinion? Let's review what we know that is factual.

- Can we consolidate and simplify this list in any way?

- You reached this decision very quickly. I'm assuming this means that there are no issues to discuss. Is that true? Are you ready to move on?

- Did everyone just hear what Rohan said? Rohan, would you please repeat your comment?

- Everyone seems to like this solution. Before you vote, let's make sure we have considered all the positive and negative implications. What are obstacles to implementation? What suggestions do you have for dealing with these obstacles?

- Luis, did Melissa answer your question? Do you have another? Does anyone have a follow-up question?

There is no list of "best" questions to ask. Each facilitator needs to make the determination of the types of questions that will help manage task and relationship issues. Asking the same questions in the same order repeatedly should be avoided, however, since this makes it appear that you are responding by rote. Listening closely is essential to determining what questions are needed.

Value of Silence. The first part of this chapter might give the impression that facilitators do a lot of talking. So let's revisit listening. Listening is the most important thing facilitators do. Facilitators who don't listen carefully miss opportunities to improve the functioning of the group. And facilitators definitely can talk too much. I was once a member of a group that had an initial meeting with a facilitator but then elected to hold the rest of our meetings informally. The facilitator offered so many process comments during our first meeting that we lost our train of thought and made very little progress on our task. In retrospect, I think the facilitator was well meaning but took too much to heart in his role in ensuring good process. Just as constantly correcting a child's grammar might cause her to lose enthusiasm for talking with you, correcting everything in a group that falls outside appropriate process is disruptive. Before you speak, decide whether what you're saying is useful.

Facilitators do speak quite a bit at the beginning of a session when process and procedures are being explained. They describe techniques and help group members move through those techniques. They close the session and make sure that everyone knows what comes next. In between, they speak when it is necessary or clarifying for them to do so. But as facilitators we should appreciate the value of silence. And in silence, we should realize that we are communicating even then.

Importance of Nonverbal Communication

"Nonverbal messages carry more weight than verbal messages" (Peltier & James, 2008, p. 62). Take for example the boss who tells subordinates to come into his office at any time but who leaves his door partially closed and has an irritated look on his face whenever someone knocks and comes in. Will people regularly come to that office? Or think about the various ways someone can say "Good job." These positive words, said with a sarcastic tone, deliver just the opposite message. The importance of meaning garnered from nonverbal communication is one of the reasons for the use of e-mail emoticons— :) [smile]; : ([frown]; ;) [wink]. We all know that spoken words convey just part of a message.

As a facilitator, you need to be aware of your own body language and that of group members. Both are important in setting a tone. And failure to notice body language in group members might lead you to make inappropriate and perhaps disastrous choices as a facilitator.

Face and Body Language

The study of face and body language is called **kinesics**. Components include eye contact, body language and movement, and facial expressions. A point needs to be emphasized here that nonverbal communication and norms of behavior vary from culture to culture and from person to person. Some people smile frequently and others rarely. Some cultures value direct eye contact; others do not. As Matsumoto (1991) says, facial expressions are "simultaneously universal and culturally specific" (p. 128).

You may have taken part in an experiment in school in which you were shown different facial expressions and asked to assess whether the person was happy, sad, angry, sad, disgusted, and other choices. Some of these, such as a person crying, seemed to have an easy answer. Others were more difficult: could you discern, for example, the difference between disgust and contempt? Technology now exists to freeze films made during trial testimony and dispositions so that micro expressions, those that are so fleeting that they cannot be observed by the naked eye, can be assessed. These brief expressions are generally thought to be reflexive and quite accurate in assessing behaviors such as truthfulness. The naked eye, however, cannot see these expressions and so we are left to make attributions or judgments about what expressions might mean.

As a facilitator, you need to be cautious about relying too much on nonverbal cues. However, an awareness of ways in which nonverbal communication may send messages is important for facilitators. Use of body language, eye contact, voice and speech patterns unrelated to words used, touch, and use of space all make statements.

Someone's facial expression, gestures, or body posture may very well reflect what he or she is feeling. There are overall cues that you can easily observe that, along with other factors, may give you some cues as to what the group as a whole is feeling. In like manner, group members may very well be influenced, knowingly or not, by the facilitator's body language and other nonverbal cues.

Eye contact. If several members are avoiding making eye contact with you or with each other, the topic under discussion may be sensitive. People may be indicating that they don't want to discuss this issue in a way similar to that in which unprepared students avoid catching the teacher's eye. Whether or not you pursue the topic and "discuss the undiscussable" depends on the importance of the topic to the purpose of the meeting and the type and context of the group. Intense eye contact or staring by one person may be viewed as hostile behavior, an attempt to intimidate, or perhaps just someone operating under a different cultural norm. Looking directly at someone is an effective way to draw the person into the discussion and/or have the person cease whatever inappropriate behavior that may be occurring. The facilitator should make it a point to make eye contact with all members in the group, without singling out certain people or directing all attention to one side of the room.

Body posture and movement. If quite a few people are shifting in their seats, stretching, or perhaps even getting up to leave the room, the group may be overdue for a break. If a physical time out is not possible, try to have people move into smaller groups or do some exercise in which they get up and move around—in other words, try for a change in activity if not an actual break. In your own posture, you want to avoid standing for long periods of time with your hands on your hips or crossed in front of your body. If you are recovering from an injury or otherwise have a need to stand up, sit down, or do anything that might be viewed as unusual, mention this briefly to the group so that your movement does not become a distraction. A facilitator can also use movement to check on the progress of small group discussions, break up pockets of non-relevant small talk that might occur, or emphasize a point.

Facial expressions. Much of what is noticed in a group setting appears on the face. We have all observed tight or phony smiles in which only the lips and no other part of the face is involved, a knitted brow, a raised eyebrow, or overall expressions of anger, surprise, or disapproval. You should pay attention to these expressions, especially in conflict situations, and use these cues, along with others, to decide on appropriate interventions. If your own face tends to be overly expressive and reflective of your emotions, you might try to emulate the "cop's face" that is sometimes mentioned in books and shows on police work. Only rooky officers betray their feelings in their facial expressions. More experienced officers learn to keep a neutral expression. Facilitators are not interrogating suspects, of course. We can, and should, display emotion, but we should try to keep our facial expressions from betraying feelings of frustration or revealing our opinion of matters under discussion. The next section addresses another manner in which nonverbal meaning is conveyed: the use of paralanguage.

Paralanguage—It's How You Say It

A popular phrase, "It's not what you say, it's how you say it," makes an important point. Never underestimate the effect of a sarcastic tone of voice. Consider this question, "Why are you here?" By placing the emphasis on a different word of the question, the meaning changes. "*Why* are you here?" asks for a reason for your presence. "Why are *you* here?" asks, "Why you instead of someone else?" "Why are you *here*?" is a question of place—"Why are you here instead of somewhere else?"

Paralanguage refers to tone of voice, volume, range, quality, articulation, rate of speech, fillers such as ums and ahs, as well as groans and sighs. If you've ever noticed a colleague sighing and groaning, you know the power of these behaviors. The pregnant pause is another paralanguage cue. If everyone in a group falls silent immediately following a comment, this silence means something. As a facilitator, you need to interpret what it means and, more importantly, decide whether you should do something about it. Novice facilitators rush to fill silence. More experienced facilitators know that waiting it out and paying close attention to what is said after a period of silence can be useful. How physical space is used is another area of nonverbal communication.

Proxemics—Use of Space

Proxemics is a term used to describe personal use of space. Again, cultural differences exist in the amount of personal space between people that is deemed comfortable. In some cultures, it is considered rude not to stand very close to someone. In the United States culture, we often back up if people crowd us. In group discussions in Western cultures, the distance between people generally runs between eighteen inches and four feet (Lumsden & Lumsden, 1993, p. 225). However, even within cultures, individuals differ in how much space they expect. You may have noticed people putting their coffee cups on one side of them and their folders on another when they first sit at a conference table. This use of markers establishes personal boundaries; people may not even be aware of these behaviors. The power allotted to people may influence how much space someone is given. Observing where and how people sit, what people sit together, and how definite people are in marking their boundaries may provide useful information. Some of these behaviors may, however, be habit and mean next to nothing. If people who have been sitting rather close together, start to back up or push themselves away from the group, this may mean a variety of things ranging from "I don't like the direction of this conversation," to "My back hurts and I need a break." Again, pay attention but not excessive attention to nonverbal cues.

Touch is an aspect of nonverbal behavior, related to personal space, that deserves special mention. Most organizations today include workshops and guidelines that describe the types of touching that could be viewed as sexual harassment.

Beyond that, people differ in their comfort levels with such things as a pat on the shoulder or a touch on the arm used to get someone's attention or to show empathy. Additionally, some cultures do not allow touching between male and female colleagues. If you ask group members to shake hands with the person on each side of them, for example, you may be asking a female member to do something that is contrary to her beliefs. In addition to being mindful of what you ask members to do, you might also make a blanket statement that group members should not hesitate to refrain from anything that is uncomfortable to them. If you work with a number of multicultural or international groups, I suggest you do some reading on different customs (see, for example, Martin & Chaney, 2006; Morrison & Conaway, 2006) and, in addition, talk with people from the cultures and countries involved if at all possible. When I ask someone from a culture about a particular custom, I may hear, "Only the older people believe that," or "That's really okay, but be sure not to do...." Many of these scenarios arise in opening exercises or when you are working as a trainer/facilitator, but assigning males and females from different cultures to work together in small groups can also give rise to awkward situations. When you have people from a variety of cultures together, you need to be particularly vigilant about nonverbal communication messages and customs.

Facilitators who have worked with groups for a number of years usually become very adept at reading the room, which is one way of saying that they are very tuned in to nonverbal communication. What people say is important, of course. Equally important to a facilitator, however, is how other members react to what the facilitator says or does. The tension and discomfort that may be apparent in their face and body language provide information that is useful in determining appropriate process choices.

Summary

Communication is a central focus of the facilitator role and as I stated at the beginning of this chapter, you cannot not communicate. As we leave this chapter, we are not leaving the topic of communication. What we say, how we communicate nonverbally, and how we react to the communication cues of others all influence our effectiveness as facilitators. We focus next on the task function: getting the job done or the purpose accomplished. In most business groups, this is of critical importance and the primary reason facilitators are brought in. Groups, left to their own devices, may deviate from the task. The facilitator is there to keep the group focused.

References

Brilhart, J. K. (1986). *Effective group discussion* (5th ed.). Dubuque, IA: W. C. Brown.

Hirokawa, R. Y. (1980). A comparative analysis of communication patterns within effective and ineffective decision-making groups. *Communication Monographs, 47,* 312–321.

Lumsden, G., & Lumsden, D. (1993). *Communicating in groups and teams: Sharing leadership.* Belmont, CA: Wadsworth.

Martin, J. S., & Chaney, L. H. (2006). *Global business etiquette. A guide to international communication and customs.* Westport, CT: Praeger.

Morrison, T., & Conaway, W. A. (2006). Kiss, bow, or shake hands (2nd ed.). Avon, MA: Adams Media.

Matsumoto, D. (1991). Cultural influences on facial expressions of emotion. *The Southern Communication Journal, 56,* 128–137.

Peltier, J. W., & James, M. L. (2008). Are future business teachers aware of gender differences? *Journal of Business and Training Education, 17,* 58–66.

Task

Key Concepts

- Starting the session
- Choice of ground rules
- Use of appropriate techniques
- Use of technology/groupware
- Keeping the group focused
- Patterns of performance
- Member task roles
- Closing the session

Helping groups get the job done is what facilitation is all about. Facilitators need to be focused, organized, and flexible… planning ahead but allowing for changes if a different direction or approach will better accomplish the goal. To do that, ideally you have many ideas and options in your toolbox. You've probably heard the phrase, "If you only have a hammer, you are always looking for a nail." If you are, however, knowledgeable about many procedures and techniques, you are able to choose among them and perhaps create a hybrid technique that will work well for your group's task.

This chapter is organized in a beginning-to-end format and assumes that you are planning a face-to-face group session. Between starting the session and closing activities, I cover the use of ground rules and appropriate techniques as well as ways to help a group maintain focus. I also describe patterns of performance and group task roles.

Starting the Session

All essential agendas and supporting materials have been distributed. You've organized the session including technology to be used, materials, supplies, and room logistics. As far as possible, you've arranged the room with an eye on the message it delivers as well as its functionality. What's left is the session itself. Here are some suggestions for getting off to a good start.

Arrive early. This allows you to make adjustments to the room, organize your materials, relax, and be ready to greet people. However, no matter how early you arrive, expect at least one participant to already be there. I've always found this to be true, and when I mention it to others, everyone agrees. View this as a positive—an opportunity to get to know one of the group members. But don't expect to have private time to write visuals and read your notes. This, very likely, won't happen.

Learn and use names. Depending on the occasion and the formality of the meeting, name tags or name tents may be waiting at the door or already distributed around the room. For a smaller meeting, you may want to bring name tents as well as markers and ask people to write their names so that you are able to address people by name during the session. Try to learn a few names before the session begins.

Begin on time. The only exception to this is extremely bad weather or an unexpected circumstance that has delayed a majority of people. Starting on time is also important after breaks and lunch. The five or ten minutes that are lost each time you begin late add up and you might find yourself not able to end the meeting on time—ending late is a sure way to have a room full of frustrated participants, no matter how well the session has gone up to that point.

Restate the purpose and review the agenda. If you have previously distributed the agenda, there should be no surprises and all that is needed is a quick restatement of the purpose and plan for the session. If members are seeing this for the first time (a situation to be avoided whenever possible), spend enough time to ensure that everyone understands the plan. Mention refreshment and break times and arrangements that have been made regarding technology use. State that you will begin on time after each break. Explain that you will leave a few seats by the door for late comers if someone is detained on a phone call. Make a point that the session is arranged so that you will accomplish your purpose in the allotted time. In some types of extended facilitation, the development of the purpose and ground rules is part of the session. Generally, however, agendas are agreed upon before the meeting.

What about introductions? Opening with introductions often is an expected procedure in a group that does not meet regularly. Before the meeting, find out if participants know each other and what brief piece of information from each person might be useful for the purpose of the session. One such introduction might be, "I'm Sue Storm, my function here is to present data from last year's survey." Do not include introductions just for your benefit. Introductions can get out of control and take precious time. You don't want 45 minutes of a three-hour meeting taken up with introductions. If people already know each other and if you have introduced yourself through materials previously sent, you can just state your name and move right into the purpose of a task-focused meeting. If, however, the group is meeting for a more social reason or if the material covered is sensitive, more time needs to be spent on developing relationships and a level of comfort among the participants. Whatever you do, you don't want to violate norms of behavior or go against what is generally done at the beginning of sessions unless you have a reason to do so. If you do, mention the reason for the deviation. People are creatures of habit.

Use opening activities wisely. Tread carefully with opening exercises. Some people really dislike these and arrive late just to avoid them. Getting-to-know-you activities, in particular, seem to have a bad reputation. For groups in which socializing is a major part of the agenda, such activities are expected and welcome. For other more task-oriented groups, such activities are suspect. However, if you begin with some kind of dyad activity that leads directly into the purpose of the day, these activities can break the ice and also give you a jump start on uncovering important issues. An example would be to have participants work in pairs to answer a question such as "What tangible forms of support do teams need from an organization?" if that is an important issue for your group. If you are working as a facilitator/trainer, you might begin with some sort of exercise that gets people engaged in your topic. I like to use agree/disagree sheets that contain a list of statements, usually about ten, related to the topic that will be under discussion. People complete the sheet alone and then discuss in pairs items on which they disagree. After sufficient time is given to go through the list, I lead a full group discussion on the list. This could take up to an hour if the items are written to allow important issues to emerge. I've found that even the most reticent participants do well with this type of opening exercise. I would consider, however, using a name other than opening activity. A few sample questions follow:

Agree/Disagree Statements

1. A large group is best if the purpose is idea generation.

2. Consensus is important and necessary for all group decisions.

3. Disagreeing with a member's idea is rude.

These statements have been written in a way that is open to interpretation. In discussing the statements (debriefing the activity), the facilitator/trainer can mention the relevant issues raised by each statement. I generally ask for a show of hands of how many agree and disagree with each statement, and then ask a few volunteers to give reasons for agreement and disagreement with each statement. Brief points for agreement and disagreement are below.

Statement 1. Agree—the more people, the more ideas generated. **Disagree**—with more people, individuals feel a lesser need to participate; ideas can get lost. A key word here is *large*—participants interpret that differently and this influences answers. A group needs to be large enough for the purpose but no larger than needed.

Statement 2. Agree—consensus is important and should be used for decisions that require commitment. **Disagree**—consensus takes time and is not necessary for routine decisions. A key word in this statement is *all*.

Statement 3. Agree—disagreement can be rude depending on what is said and how it is said. **Disagree**—disagreement on issues is important and should not be considered rude if statements are not personal. A key word here is *idea*.

Although ground rules have implications for both task and relationship, I am discussing them here since they are generally either included as part of the agenda or discussed right after the opening of the meeting.

Choice of Ground Rules

In Chapter 2, I talked about organizational norms of behavior as an input variable that influences group process and outcome. Groups also have norms of behavior that have an influence on interaction, process, and effectiveness. Everyone always being on time to meetings is a group norm. Interrupting each other, unfortunately, may be another group norm. Being highly productive and effective or just doing enough to get by are other examples of group norms. For better or worse, groups that meet over a period of time have established ways or working. In newly established or one-time groups, facilitators have a chance to encourage norms of behavior that are appropriate given the purpose and function of the group. In long-term groups, facilitators need to understand that existing norms may be difficult to change.

Ground rules are a more formalized statement of norms of behavior that are used by the group to improve group functioning. For short meetings, I like to have ground rules for the session printed on the agenda that has already been distributed and also posted on a flip chart that is visible during the session. For most one-time sessions, this list can be quite brief. If these ground rules have "face validity"—i.e., nothing seems unusual or unexpected—there is no need for a long discussion of the rules. You may also call them something else if you think people will react negatively to "rules." I sometimes refer to them as process goals. In one session that involved a number of community residents discussing an agreed-upon topic in small groups situated around a large room, the following **process goals** were printed at the top of each agenda:

- Everyone participates.
- All ideas raised are given appropriate consideration and discussion.
- Groups stay on task.

These goals worked well in this situation. I would not use "everyone participates" as a ground rule, but as a goal, it established a climate of open discussion. Some of the facilitators in this situation were inexperienced and had received only brief training. The goals were as much for their benefit as for the participants'. I suggested that all members use the process goals to keep the group conversation going on track. This took some of the pressure off the neophyte facilitators and also ended up working very well with this congenial group of people. In fact, I heard later that individuals in the group said things like, "I've been talking too long, what do the rest of you think?" Even experienced facilitators may find that group members can monitor each other if they agree on the ground rules and see their relevance. In certain situations, especially those involving substantial conflict or long-term discussions, participants may develop the ground rules with input from the facilitator. This is discussed further in Chapter 9.

Ground rules should be appropriate for the group and the situation, as shown in Exhibit 6-1.

Exhibit 6-1. Typical Ground Rules

❖ Stay on task.

❖ Criticize issues, not people.

❖ Avoid blaming language. Use **I,** not **you.**

❖ Allow people to speak without interruption.

❖ Use all relevant data.

❖ Separate fact from opinion.

❖ Focus on interests, not positions.

An example of blaming language is, "You're not making sense." This choice of words may make the speaker defensive. If you, instead, put the blame on yourself and say, "I don't understand the distinction you're making," the same purpose is accomplished without making the person feel defensive.

You may also want to add or discuss procedural ground rules such as "turn off all cell phones and pagers," but at this point, this statement should be a reminder of something that has already been discussed. Otherwise, a discussion of the merits of this rule could take a good portion of the time allotted for your session.

In developmental groups, a discussion of ground rules can take a considerable amount of time, and the ground rules may be more detailed. Schwartz (2002) suggests the following:

- Test assumptions and inferences.
- Share all relevant information.
- Use specific examples and agree on what important words mean.
- Explain your reasons and intent.
- Focus on interests, not positions.
- Combine advocacy and inquiry.

- Jointly design next steps and ways to test disagreements.
- Discuss undiscussable issues.
- Use a decision-making rule that generates the level of commitment needed.

Although many ground rules are generic and all-purpose, others may be added for specific situations or types of groups. Usually a facilitator proposes a short list and asks members if there is any discussion or addition before moving on. When we turn to the chapters on decision-making and problem-solving techniques, you will see that some techniques have ground rules imbedded in the process such as fully describing the problem before attempting to solve it or using brainstorming to stimulate creativity.

Use of Appropriate Techniques

A well-crafted agenda is one way to keep the group focused on the purpose of the session. The agenda may or may not include a running timeline for the session as discussed in Chapter 4. In any case, the facilitator needs to be very aware of time. Failure to do so will result in a very rushed ending to a session or, more likely, failure to accomplish whatever was planned and expected. I can remember a discussion with a facilitator whose group failed to accomplish its purpose. I asked, "What happened?"

The response was that the group members were having a good time discussing something else that came up (unrelated to the point of the session), and the facilitator thought that it was important to let them have this discussion. As a result, a follow-up meeting needed to be scheduled to accomplish the original purpose. Keeping the group focused can be a challenge. Use of specific techniques can help a group accomplish its purpose.

There are many approaches to group decision making and problem solving and several options to the use of open discussion. At times, just having a discussion with ground rules is sufficient to accomplish the purpose. Other times, the nature of the decision or problem or the makeup of the group calls for a more structured approach. The choice of approach could be critical to the success of the session. Chapter 11 explains principles of the problem-solving process and reasons for use of specific techniques; Chapters 12, 13, and 14 cover techniques that can be used for specific purposes. In this book, I use the term "technique" for a procedure that has a name and a person credited with development of the technique and a formalized process that generally includes a set number of steps. I use the term "procedure" for other tools such as agendas and ground rules. Techniques not only give structure to the process but they allow for management of people issues. In Nominal Group Technique (Chapter 12), for example, everyone has an equal voice and voting is private. This is especially good in groups that have significant status differences or that involve discussion of sensitive issues.

First, of course, whatever technique or approach chosen must be acceptable to the group. A very creative group is apt to resist and feel constrained by the use of a mathematical procedure such as Kepner-Tregoe (Chapter 12), although they might see the value of it if the purpose is explained. Similarly, groups that are used to very linear decision-making processes such as Fishbone (Chapter 13) might be frustrated if an approach such as Appreciative Inquiry (Chapter 14) were introduced, especially without notice. Keep the group in mind. The more the approach you want to use deviates from common practice in a group, the more important it is to send out advance information giving reasons and allowing participants feedback into the plan for the day.

Use your creativity and perhaps a hybrid approach to craft a technique that allows for group preferences. Insert a bit of creativity or positive imagery into a process that is familiar to the group if you believe doing so will result in a better process for the purpose. Be cautious about becoming especially fond of one process. The danger is that you then begin to force this technique on every situation. To the best of your ability, view each situation as a blank slate and consider what would work best for that group. I describe each of the techniques mentioned above as well as other techniques in later chapters. Although the majority of meetings today still run using low-tech options such as whiteboards and flip charts, you may find yourself in a situation that calls for technology and perhaps groupware.

Use of Technology/Groupware

If you are using technology to facilitate decision making, be sure that you have practiced using the technology or, even better, that specialists trained in the system will be on hand to manage the technical aspects of the process. I advise against attempting to handle both facilitation and technology unless this is a particular specialty of yours. Most of us have stories of meetings or sessions that we have attended in which the technology did not work. If something does not work after a few minutes, move on and use low-tech materials if that is at all possible. If the entire meeting is planned around the use of a specific technology, such as a group decision support system (GDSS), now generally called group support system (GSS), then do everything in your power to ensure that technology will work as expected. Many meeting facilities have rooms devoted to GSS, and an electronic meeting support system is what many people visualize when group technology is mentioned.

Groupware is now used as a generic term to refer to hardware, software, and services that support face-to-face and virtual teams (Coovert & Thompson, 2001). Since these terms are a bit confusing, some history might help. Initial work on GDSS began over 20 years ago and initially focused on using a network of computers to allow members to participate in idea generation and to vote on alternative decisions (Andriessen, 2003). This interest expanded to include an examination of computer-supported cooperative work (CSCW), which is "concerned with how technology can help people work together more effectively" whether they are face-to-face or at a distance (Coovert & Thompson, 2001, p. 2). CSCW generally focuses on groups of 10 or fewer. Eventually the D in GDSS was dropped to reflect an enlarged focus on technologies beyond the initial electronic support systems. Thus GDSS became group support system (GSS). Despite differences in focus between GSS and CSCW, both now use the term "groupware" (Grudin & Poltrock, 1997).

Technology to facilitate group interaction and task accomplishment is plentiful and offers both advantages and disadvantages. These depend, of course, on the extent to which groups use technology to accomplish their goals and the expertise with which it is used. Advantages include improved accessibility of information, increased information-processing capabilities, and inclusion of members across boundaries of time and space. Disadvantages include loss of communication cues that are available in face-to-face meetings and the resultant loss of richness of information (Daft & Lengel, 1986; Hollingshead & McGrath, 1995). The types of technology that are both available and popular change from month to month. Scott (2003) in discussing communication technology as related to groups and teams says, "What is new today may not be new tomorrow" (p. 135). He mentions four major categories of communication technology most commonly used by groups and teams and gives examples of each: (1) routine group communication technology (listservs, voice mail, instant messaging); (2) meeting/project systems (audio conferencing, audio/ video conferencing, group decision support systems); (3) document management/storage technologies (word processing tools useful for group writing and editing; and (4) coordination/collaboration tools (group calendars and a variety of groupware and conferencing systems). For a more complete review of collaborative technologies, see Jones and Ruona (2006).

If you are using technology during a face-to-face meeting, even if it is just the use of slides for presentation of material in a dual trainer/facilitator role, be certain that the technology works well with the room arrangement and that everyone can see the screen. Use of electronic slides adds a note of formality to the proceedings and also may inhibit discussions, especially if lighting is dimmed. Present in an interactive manner and be careful not to block the view of participants. A poster, flip chart, or handout works well to explain the steps of a technique and eliminates the need to display this information electronically.

Whatever aids you use should work well with the size and seating arrangement of the group. Test this ahead of time if possible and make adjustments if the room is not as you expected. In a large room with a group size over 25, you might want to have several flip charts with easels positioned around the room. Recording ideas helps groups focus. This easy low-tech solution works well to collect ideas. I discuss suggestions to encourage creativity in groups in Chapter 10 and techniques to use for generation of ideas in Chapter 12. Don't allow technology and the aids you use to become anything other than tools. Keep an open mind, consider what is available, and choose the low-tech or high-tech solutions that will work best either singularly or in combination to meet the needs of your group. Whatever you choose, a primary role of the facilitator is to keep the group focused.

Keeping the Group Focused

Keeping the group on task is considered a primary function of a group facilitator. In addition to implementing a stay-on-task ground rule, there are other tools and procedures that can help keep a group focused. One of the first things a decision-making group should decide is the desired level of agreement that constitutes an acceptable decision outcome. Deciding this first not only saves time later on but it separates the decision rule from the topic—and from emotions that might emerge from a discussion of the topic.

Decide on decision rule. A decision on the level of agreement/commitment needed has ramifications for the type of specific technique that might be used and the time devoted to the process. If a group meets regularly and has established a norm of reaching agreement on a decision (for example, majority rule), then this norm only needs to be stated and confirmed. Otherwise, members should discuss what level of agreement is needed. If a decision ranks high on importance and commitment desired, then consensus is the likely choice. **Consensus** implies that all group members agree with and are committed to a decision. Although this does not need to be, and rarely is, total agreement or commitment, it should be a decision that all can accept and a level of commitment that goes beyond tolerance. Thus, consensus might mean that all agree that this decision is one they can support. **Voting** may occur on rather routine decisions, when the topic is sensitive, or on occasions in which groups don't believe consensus is necessary or possible. Voting by each member can be private and anonymous (using slips of paper) or by a show of hands. Whatever method is chosen, members need to agree ahead of time whether a **simple majority or two-thirds vote** is needed for the process to end and the decision to stand. As discussed earlier, you as the process facilitator do not have a vote on decisions unless you are working in a leader/facilitator role.

Record ideas. Many images of meetings show a person writing on a flip chart standing in front of other people who are seated. This person may be a facilitator or someone charged with the task of recording ideas. Recording ideas as they are mentioned provides a record, encourages participation, and keeps the group on track. In a group of more than 15 or 20, you may want people to work in small groups to generate lists that are then shared with the entire session. In this manner, you can move the group toward selection of viable ideas. Posting completed flip chart sheets around the room is a way to maintain focus. Put a heading on each sheet and display them in order to enable readers to follow the progression of ideas from initial development to detailed plans.

Use parking lot. Another procedure for keeping the group on track involves the use of a parking lot. This simply involves drawing a square on a board, flip chart, computer screen, or poster paper and listing issues there that emerge throughout the session that, although important and interesting, are not related to the task at hand. Explain early on how this will be used. When you mention the "stay on task" ground rule, it is easy enough to explain that unrelated items of importance that arise will be listed in the parking lot. The question becomes, of course, what happens to these issues? There are several choices. One is to come back to them later in the session if time allows. Another choice, and one I favor, is to state that a listing of these items will be distributed to members—perhaps to management, depending on the purpose of the meeting—so that can be addressed at a later time. In my experience, people are satisfied with this. A visible parking lot makes the point that staying on task is important. If someone disagrees with the placement of their item on this list, ask the person to make a case either immediately or at a later time that the issue is germane to the discussion. If members agree that the point is directly related to the issue at hand, then it can be removed from the parking lot and discussed. The parking lot can also be used to remind the facilitator and the group of an issue raised that is not relevant now but will be later on in the session. If the group does not like the "parking lot" name, use a different title such as "ideas for later discussion." The name does not matter. Having a place to list ideas that need to be put aside for a while is a valuable procedure for maintaining focus.

Collect feedback. Another way to maintain focus is to ask for feedback throughout the day if it is a day-long session or right before break in a shorter session.

This may be a quick question of how satisfied people are with the direction and activities of the session thus far, a response to a task or process question, or simply what issue on the board they want to tackle next. I keep small pieces of paper and index cards available for this purpose. Another technique is to have an **ideas and comments** flip chart posted at the side of the room. People may write whatever they want on this sheet as the day progresses. In my opinion, this is used best as a type of parking lot that is under the control of the group. Thoughts and ideas that people want captured can go here. Members have opportunities to write something on their way to or from breaks. The facilitator needs to read this as the day progresses to see if anything written there affects the plan or process for the day. At the end of the session and in the manner that has been previously agreed upon, items on the flip chart will be shared with the group.

Adapt as necessary. If you have had an opportunity to ask the questions covered in Chapter 4, you should have a clear idea of what can be accomplished during the facilitated session. If members were involved in the planning, there should be clear expectations all around. At times, however, unexpected issues arise or something occurs that raises the question of whether the expected outcome is still possible or whether the group's interest is better served by an alternative approach. Once it is clear that issues being raised—issues that are relevant to the issue at hand—are more complex than anticipated, or something else arises that will take substantial time to address, you need to ask the members whether they agree to a change in plan. If so, then what is the altered desired outcome for the session?

Of course, people not at the session may not be pleased with this altered outcome, so be prepared for others to question your judgment. If you have been at fault, for example, by encouraging the group to discuss unrelated issues that led away from the planned outcome, you may need to offer your services to complete the original task. We all want to avoid such situations. People who balk at answering facilitator questions during advance planning should be reminded that the purpose of such planning is to ensure that time during the session is used wisely and that desired outcomes are realistic. But things happen. Staying with a plan when other more important and related issues arise is unprofessional and most likely not even possible. Advance planning that includes participants should keep these situations to a minimum.

Although keeping the group on task is considered a primary function of a facilitator, this task, especially in long-term groups, does not include a step-by-step progression toward an outcome.

Patterns of Performance

Tuckman and Jensen (1977) identified five stages of development that describe typical process for many groups:

- **Forming:** Initial stage; orientation; getting to know each other
- **Storming:** Disagreement among members; conflict; dissatisfaction
- **Norming:** Cohesiveness; development of group structure; establishment of norms, roles, and relationships
- **Performing:** Focus on actual task; getting the job done
- **Adjourning:** Final stage; task is finished; saying goodbye

Because these stages are easy to remember, they are commonly cited and serve to give an overall understanding of how groups progress toward a goal. We should not expect all groups to go through these stages in this order or to spend the same length of time in each stage. Additionally, Poole and Baldwin (1996) caution against focusing too much on any established set of phases or steps that a group may follow.

There are interesting patterns, however. Gersick (1988) observed a variety of types of task-oriented long-standing teams and found that all teams experienced **punctuated equilibrium**—"periods of inertia broken by bursts of energy and change. For each team, precisely at the midpoint of its life, a period of crisis stuck" (Lumsden & Lumsden, 1993, pp. 94–95). This is similar to processes described in Chapter 10 related to creativity. Things don't move in a straight line. Gersick reported a period of getting down to business punctuated by a midpoint of some type of crisis or disruption. I've noticed the same thing with groups working on tasks requiring substantial effort. Often a break of some kind is needed. If we as facilitators do not expect our long-term groups to move forward in a straight line from beginning to end, we might all be more relaxed about the process. Being aware of changes in process and performance that occur over the years in long-term groups (Katz, 1988) also will help us adapt our actions to meet group needs.

Members in the group also perform roles that help the group stay focused. These are covered in the next section.

Member Task Roles

I mentioned in earlier chapters that research from over 60 years ago (Benne & Sheats, 1948) is still valid and still used today in terms of the roles members play in groups. The three types of roles identified are task, maintenance, and individual or self-centered. Task roles help groups accomplish goals, maintenance roles promote social support and positive relationships among members and self-centered roles promote individual goals and may work against the accomplishment of group goals. Task goals are listed below. Maintenance and self-centered roles are discussed in the next chapter. Knowledge of these roles will contribute to your understanding of how groups work. You will recognize them as similar to roles performed by facilitators.

Exhibit 6-2. Group Member Task Roles

Initiator: Makes suggestions, contributes new ideas, recommends goals and procedures

Information seeker: Asks for facts, experiences, and ideas; seeks clarification

Information giver: Offers facts, experiences, and ideas; identifies relevant data

Elaborator: Works with suggestions already offered; provides examples

Opinion seeker: Seeks opinions, values, beliefs of others, especially about course of action

Opinion giver: Gives own opinions, values, beliefs, especially about course of action

Orienter: Relates what is happening to the goals; summarizes ideas and suggestions

Coordinator: Provides linkages between ideas and suggestions; ties things together

Energizer: Encourages the group to increased activity and higher accomplishment

Evaluator: Applies some standard to judge the accomplishment to the group

Procedural technician: Distributes handouts; pays attention to logistics

Recorder: Takes notes

Source: Benne, K., & Sheats, P. (1948). Functional roles of group members, *Journal of Social Issues, 4,* 41–49.

As has been discussed, as a facilitator you model appropriate ways of communicating in groups. If you are working as a facilitator/trainer, you may want to talk about these roles and have members identify which roles they generally play. Encourage members to become involved in a way that best suits them.

Closing the Session

If you manage your time carefully throughout the session, there should be no need to rush at the end when everyone (including yourself) may be tired and less willing to engage in thoughtful discussion. Ideally, you will come to the result that was agreed upon ahead of time (for example, reach a decision or clearly define criteria that will be used in step two of decision making). Following that, closing activities should be brief.

Next steps? Everyone in the room and the people who hired you should all agree on the desired outcome of this session and what comes next. Spend closing time reminding people what will happen to the materials generated today, the decisions that were made, and what each person is expected to do as follow up. Make clear your next step if you are involved in further activities.

Evaluation/feedback. Ask ahead of time if the company has a prepared form that they use for session feedback. Although this is expected for training sessions, some companies use them for other types of sessions that have invited facilitators or speakers. If not, bring your own and collect brief feedback on each participant's views of the session. A sample is below. Keep the form brief. Questions such as "What went well?" and "What would we do differently?" are good ones. Your opening line is a chance to personalize the form for the group.

Exhibit 6-3. Sample Evaluation Form

Your honest ratings and comments on this session will help us plan future sessions. Using a scale of 1 (lowest) to 10 (highest), please provide a number that best describes your response to each of the following four questions:

1. I understood the purpose of the session.   _____

2. I believe the purpose was accomplished.   _____

3. Time was used well.   _____

4. The atmosphere of the session encouraged   _____
   participation.

Short-answer questions:

5. What was the best thing about this session?

   _____

   _____

   _____

6. What one thing would you change?

   _____

   _____

   _____

7. What suggestions do you have for future sessions of this type?

   _____

   _____

   _____

Thank you for your feedback.

A shorter form with only a few questions such as "Best thing about this session?" and "What I would change?" can also be used for brief sessions. As with everything else, the feedback asked for at the end should fit the context of the group. If the form is too long, people won't complete it or will simply mark responses without paying much attention.

I try to spend some time after a session reflecting on what I thought went well or perhaps did not. If I worked with a co-facilitator, we attempt to do this as soon as possible after completion of the session—right after is best, perhaps in conjunction with reading the feedback forms. This brief amount of time is well spent, particularly if you plan to continue to work with the group.

Summary

Getting the job done is the primary purpose of most task-oriented groups. Even relationship-focused groups have some task aspects. In this chapter, I've covered the process from getting started to closing the meeting and collecting feedback. Sections on the use of ground rules and appropriate techniques and ways to help a group maintain focus are included. I also described patterns of performance over time and group task roles. The next chapter focuses on building relationships and climate.

References

Andriessen, J. H. E. (2003). *Working with groupware.* London: Springer.

Benne, K., & Sheats, P. (1948). Functional roles of group members, *Journal of Social Issues, 4,* 41–49.

Coovert, M. D., & Thompson, L. F. (2001). *Computer supported cooperative work.* Thousand Oaks, CA: Sage.

Daft, R. L., & Lengel, R. H. (1986). Organizational information requirements, media richness, and structural design. *Management Science, 32,* 554–571.

Gersick, C. J. G. (1988). Time and transition in work teams: Toward a new model of group development. *Academy of Management Journal, 31,* 9–41.

Grudin, J., & Poltrock, S. E. (1997). Computer-supported cooperative work and groupware. In M. V. Zelkowitz (Ed.), *Advances in computers* (Vol. *45,* pp. 269–320). San Diego, CA: Academic Press.

Hollingshead, A. B., & McGrath, J. E. (1995). Computer-assisted groups: A critical review of the empirical research. In R. A. Guzzo & E. Salas & Associates (Eds.), *Team effectiveness and decision making in organization* (pp. 46–78). San Francisco, CA: Jossey-Bass.

Jones, R. S., & Ruona, W.E.A. (2006). Technology's ability to facilitate virtual work: A promise unrealized or a misguided effort? In F. Nafukho and H. Chen (Eds.), *2006 Conference Proceedings of the Academy of Human Resource Development* (pp. 1394–1399). Bowling Green, OH: The Academy of Human Resource Development.

Katz, R. (1988). High performance research teams. In R. Katz (Ed.), *Managing professionals in innovative organizations* (pp. 315–324). Cambridge, MA: Ballinger.

Lumsden, G., & Lumsden, D. (1993). *Communicating in groups and teams*. Belmont, CA: Wadsworth.

Poole, M. S., & Baldwin, C. L. (1996). Developmental processes in group decision making. In R. Y. Hirokawa & M. S. Poole (Eds.), *Communication and group decision making* (2nd ed., pp. 215–241). Thousand Oaks, CA: Sage.

Schwartz, R. (2002). *The skilled facilitator* (rev. ed.). San Francisco, CA: Jossey-Bass.

Scott, C. R. (2003). New communication technology and teams. In R. Y. Hirokawa, R. S. Cathcart, L. A. Samovar, and L. D. Henman (Eds.), *Small group communication: Theory and practice* (pp. 134–147). Los Angeles, CA: Roxbury.

Tuckman, B. W., & Jensen, M. A. (1977). Stages of small group development revisited. *Group & Organization Management, 2*, 419–427.

Relationships and Climate

Key Concepts

- Creating a supportive climate
- Encouraging group involvement and ownership
- Monitoring group dynamics
- Member relationship roles
- Identifying and handling dysfunctional behaviors
- Facilitator preferences

Relationships/climate and task are the two primary components of group work. Communication skills are essential for accomplishing both. Every group has task and relationship issues; the trick is finding the balance for each group. Relationships and climate are both of critical importance in social support groups. People won't return to such groups if they don't feel comfortable. Even in the most task-centered business group, however, relationship and climate issues are important. In this chapter, I talk about creating a supportive climate and then move on to the related issue of encouraging group involvement and ownership. Group dynamics involves the management of interaction, which is a big part of relationship and climate. I end with a discussion of relationship and self-centered and dysfunctional group roles. I begin this chapter by talking about climate since climate sets the stage for relationship development.

Creating a Supportive Climate

Climate in terms of groups and group work generally refers to a supportive atmosphere in which members feel comfortable. Scheerhorn and Geist (1997) define climate as "group members' perceptions of the relative warmth or coldness that characterize the interpersonal relationships among members.

There is a reciprocal influence between the climate of a group and the task and social communication that goes on in that group" (p. 91). Larson and LaFasto (1989), in a three-year study of highly effective teams, found that (1) collaborative climate was an essential component of working well together and (2) working well together was a primary ingredient in team success. Thus, it is no surprise that creating a supportive climate is an important facilitator competency. But how do we accomplish that? Again, from the Larson and LaFasto research, people who were asked to define collaborative climate almost always mentioned **trust**.

"Trust is produced in a climate that includes four elements: (1) honesty—integrity, no lies, no exaggerations; (2) openness—a willingness to share and a receptivity to information, perceptions, ideas; (3) consistency—predictable behavior and responses; and (4) respect—treating people with dignity and fairness" (Larson & LaFasto, 1989, p. 85).

Let's relate these elements to facilitated groups. Three of them—honesty, openness, and respect—are relevant for all groups, whether they meet once or over a period of time. Consistency is more important in extended teamwork situations in which members have a continuing relationship. Trust and collaboration seem to go hand in hand. This makes sense. If group members are discussing a sensitive issue, they need to trust that others in the group will be honest and open in expressing their own views and also respectful of the views of other people. The more members trust each other, the more willing they will be to have the type of discussion that is likely to result in effective decision making.

The facilitator encourages the development of this climate by modeling appropriate behavior. Respect is certainly at the top of the list. People in a group can be expected to refrain from expressing negative personal comments when people offer ideas and opinions. Honesty and openness are more difficult and are influenced, often quite heavily, by organizational culture and the history of the individuals at the meeting. If

106

people feel threatened in some way or believe that they are putting themselves or their colleagues at risk by speaking openly about an issue, openness and honesty may be unrealistic expectations.

Remember the questions discussed in Chapter 4. The more advance information you have, the more you can plan strategies and techniques that can help mitigate a lack of trust. You may choose to use a discussion technique that allows individuals to privately raise issues that are then posted for the group. If a discussion starts out with some honest statements but then seems to be veering off course, you may ask members to privately answer a question such as, "What in your opinion is keeping the group from moving forward with this issue?" or another question that members might answer more honestly if their responses are not associated with their names. You can then have the group take a short break while you list all the responses on a flip chart. The important thing is to choose techniques that are appropriate for the situation at hand. In extended facilitation, you have an opportunity to build trust.

Importance of communication. A facilitator models respect or disrespect by the way in which he or she communicates both verbally and nonverbally with each person, the ground rules that are chosen and enforced, the humor that is used throughout the session, and the techniques and procedures that are implemented. The importance of communication in creating a supportive climate was recognized 50 years ago (Gibb, 1961). His research relates to how communication acts and responses lead to either supportive or defensive climates. He said that **defensive behavior** "occurs when an individual perceives threat or anticipates threat in the group" (p. 141). The effect of defensive behavior is hostility. **Supportive behavior**, on the other hand, allows recipients of messages to "become better able to concentrate upon the structure, the content, and the cognitive meanings of the message" (p. 141). Gibb identified six communication behaviors that tend to increase supportiveness:

1. Describes without judgment
2. Focuses on problem orientation and emphasizes mutual interests
3. Is spontaneously open and honest and not concerned with strategy
4. Conveys empathy and concern
5. Conveys equality by valuing others and their ideas
6. Engages in provisionalism, where points of view are sought and considered.

Of these, only empathy and concern have not been previously discussed. Empathy involves learning to understand what another person is feeling. Empathy does not mean that you agree with the other person, simply that you understand or try to understand why the person is behaving in a certain way. Part of an atmosphere of trust is belief that other people will respect and try to understand your feelings and concerns. Someone who feels that group members are judging what is said and not really valuing opinions expressed by other people is unlikely to be willing to take a chance and make an honest remark. Social support of members for one another contributes to climate.

Social support. Social support is interaction that is designed to communicate caring and contribute to the well-being of others (Burleson, Albrecht, Goldsmith, & Sarason, 1994). Six interrelated supportive functions served by everyday talk in a group were described by Barnes and Duck (1994) and expanded upon by Scheerhorn and Geist (1997). These functions are information, detection, ventilation, distraction, perpetuation, and regulation. Through conversation we pick up information about group members; detect signals that provide cues about someone's emotional state; give opportunities for members to vent about problems, worries, and stress; allow people to distance themselves from stress by not talking about the issue or event that is stressful; promote relationships and build group history by talking about fairly trivial details about group work and poking humor at group practices; and manage concerns about acceptance, autonomy, and self-presentation by allowing members to ease into discussion of a real problem. These behaviors work together to build a supportive climate.

Synergy and rapport. The first chapter of this book ended with a discussion of synergy—what happens when the combined efforts of individuals working together equals more than the sum of each individual working alone. Wright (2005) spoke of the importance of building relationship skills among members. Gilley, Morris, Waite, Coates, and Veliquette (2010) reference Wright in discussing the importance of relationships to the development of a "positive, comfortable, and nonthreatening communication climate with others—one that encourages other people to discuss organizational issues, problems and other ideas openly and honestly, without fear of reprisal" (p. 23). Earlier work by Gilley and Boughton (1996) related this climate to the establishment of conditions that expedite the synergistic relationship process. In this process, individuals work interdependently toward a common goal that provides opportunities for both individual and organizational growth and development. Gilley et al. (2010, pp. 23–24) state, "The outcome of a positive (synergistic) relationship between individuals is known as rapport, which is the unconditional regard for one another and is further defined as a deep concern for the well-being of others (Whichard & Kees, 2006)." Rapport engenders trust, which is an underpinning for collaborative climate.

Realistic expectations. You may be thinking—I have a three-hour session planned with people I don't know. How much influence can I have on the climate? What are realistic expectations? There are some things you can do, even in a short session, to contribute to climate. You can be clear about expectations for the session, set appropriate workable ground rules that suit the purpose of the group, and model a respectful way of speaking to and responding to others. Humor can help in enforcing ground rules. You might find a way to hold up a sign that says "Rule 3" if someone goes way off topic and violates a ground rule of staying focused. How facilitators use humor depends on how well they know the people, how comfortable they are with humor, and how appropriate they feel it is for the situation at hand.

You should never use humor if it does not feel right to you. Instead of trying to be funny, develop a climate that encourages light-hearted interaction among members. Be very careful with sarcasm. Even in the most well-intended situations, sarcasm can backfire and be misinterpreted. More importantly, it can bring conversation to a halt and drastically alter the mood of a room. Above all, a facilitator needs to show respect for the individuals in the room and for the topic under discussion. A one-time meeting with a group cannot be expected to affect climate in any lasting way, but a facilitator can establish a workable atmosphere that allows the day's task to be accomplished.

Encouraging Group Involvement and Ownership

If a supportive climate has been established, barriers to participation have been reduced. Involvement can be further encouraged by the procedures and techniques discussed in the previous chapter. Choose ground rules and techniques that reduce domination of the groups by one of two members. From Chapter 5, model verbal and nonverbal communication practices that encourage individual members to speak up and offer their ideas and suggestions.

As in the development of supportive climate, member willingness to become involved with and feel ownership for the group task stems from trust. Trust in this case has two facets: trust in the purpose and outcome of the group task and trust in one another (the latter comes from development of interpersonal relationships). Trust can be conceptualized as a willingness to be vulnerable to another (Mayer, Davis, & Schoorman, 1995). Jones, Couch, and Scott (1997) suggest that trust is an aspect of all human relations and interactions. In groups, trust encourages the development of collaborative behavior, reduces interpersonal conflict, and, in general, has a positive effect on group process and functioning.

According to McAllister (1995), interpersonal trust has cognitive and affective foundations and is cognition based in that we make decisions on whom we trust based on sound reasons and evidence that the person is trustworthy. On the other hand, trust could be generated from emotional bonds that develop between individuals (Lewis & Weigert, 1985). Pennings and Woiceshyn (1987) agree that people make emotional decisions in a trust relationship and that the emotional ties that link individuals can be the basis for interpersonal trust. As individual group members develop relationships, these relationships encourage overall levels of trust within the group to rise.

Ownership of the task further implies that members believe the group and the group outcome are important and relevant. Although the facilitator is in charge of managing group process and helping the group to accomplish its task, the process itself and the outcome of the process belongs to the members. This starts with involvement of members prior to the facilitated session. The more members are involved in planning goals and setting the agenda, the greater the likelihood that they will feel ownership of and involvement in the purpose and process of the session. As mentioned in Chapter 4, much of what happens in the early stages of planning for facilitation determines the success of any group activity. If the group is not supported by the organization and, most especially, if members do not believe that anything substantive will happen as a result of their efforts, developing feelings of ownership will be difficult if not impossible. In a similar manner, if what is planned is important to the organization but members don't see the relevance to themselves or to their day-to-day work, again ownership will be missing.

111

Involvement and ownership, then, stem from both external and internal components or sources. Internally, relationships among group members that lead to trust can facilitate development of a collaborative climate that, in turn, encourages involvement and ownership. This only happens, however, if members come into the group with at least some level of commitment and trust in the value of what they are being asked to do—the external component. Without that, without the inputs mentioned in Chapter 1, involvement and ownership are highly questionable.

An effective facilitator will do whatever is possible to encourage inputs that facilitate effective process and lead to a successful outcome for the group. The importance of a group leader in maintaining linkages between the group and external sources of support and resources has been well documented in research (Ancona, 1990; Kolb, 1996; Thamhain & Wilemon, 1988). These external linkages are sometimes called boundary activities (Ancona & Caldwell, 1990). Although the facilitator usually is not the leader of the group, the linkage role is still relevant. How relevant depends on the length and type of relationship you have with a group or team. A facilitator in certain circumstances may work with management to increase levels of commitment and allotment of resources, the amount of time devoted to a project, and/or the availability of necessary information. Such conversations, unfortunately, may also involve giving a professional opinion that what is desired will not happen given the projected group inputs. A fairly common refrain from facilitators is, "If I had known..., I would have done things differently." Issues of commitment, involvement, and ownership reinforce the importance of considering groups in context and as an open system with factors inside and outside the group affecting group process and outcome. Given group needs and limitations imposed on the group, a facilitator does the best job possible to create a process and a climate that encourage accomplishment of the group task.

Monitoring Group Dynamics

Group dynamics has to do with managing member interactions and encouraging behaviors that have a positive influence on group process. This involves using ground rules to encourage members to improve their group communication and interaction skills.

Using ground rules. The following are three examples of ground rules given in the previous chapter. For each, I give possible facilitator responses to "correct" the initial behavior that was in opposition to a specific ground rule. As the facilitator models behaviors that facilitate effective group process, members should begin to monitor themselves. As you read through this sample dialogue, consider how you would respond to each case.

Stay on task:

> **Mary:** (Makes a statement that is totally off-task)
>
> **Facilitator:** Mary, are you suggesting a different topic for discussion? Right now we are talking about X.
>
> **Mary:** No.
>
> **Facilitator:** Perhaps the relevance of your comment just isn't clear to me. Remember our ground rule to stay on task.
>
> **Mary:** Okay. It isn't relevant right now.
>
> **Facilitator:** I'll write it on the parking lot so that we won't forget your idea. You said Y, is that right?

Separate fact from opinion:

Joshua: That's a crazy idea.

Facilitator: What's the reason for your opinion, Joshua?

Joshua: I don't think the timeline works.

Facilitator: Okay—that's a statement we can work with. What information do we have about the timeline?

Allow people to speak without interruption:

Don: (Interrupting Hong)

Facilitator: Don, please allow Hong to finish her statement. Then you can respond.
Or
(Allow Don to finish his statement and then say...)

Facilitator: Hong, would you please complete your thought.

Interruptions are a common occurrence in groups. When someone interrupts, return as soon as possible to the person who was speaking before the interruption occurred. You don't want to reinforce or reward the person who interrupted by allowing that person, in this case, Don, to hold the floor. If interruption happens frequently in a group, you might want to return to the ground rule and ask members if they agree that not interrupting is important. If they do, ask members to indicate when someone has interrupted by raising their hands or by some other means that will help people break this habit. Group members generally have some fun with this, and the facilitator can then concentrate on other things. In extreme cases or when you feel a need for the group to slow down its speed of communication, you might pass a coin or some other object to the person speaking. People do not speak unless they are holding the object. Use this only for a short period of time and for a specific purpose.

Giving feedback. By giving feedback on group process, as in the example above, the facilitator is helping members improve their skills. The extent to which this is done depends on the purpose of the facilitation, the time allotted to the group meeting, and your role. You need to determine each time you intervene or take an action regarding ground rules whether your action serves a positive purpose. In a group that meets only once for a short time, too much focus on ground rules will frustrate everyone and have a negative effect on group process. People will simply stop talking. You might want to wait until a break in the discussion and then reemphasize ground rules before beginning again. In a short-term group, a few rules that everyone supports are more useful than a long list that is too time consuming to enforce.

As with the task roles mentioned in the previous chapter, Benne and Sheats (1948) also identified group maintenance or relationship roles. These roles have an effect on group dynamics and on climate and relationship development. Following this list, I discuss their third list, that of self-centered roles. In short-term groups, you won't want to call attention to these roles and make members self-conscious, but you can encourage the positive roles and discourage the negative or dysfunctional roles when you notice them.

Member Relationship (Maintenance) Roles

You may note that some of the roles from Benne and Sheat's research have similarities to facilitation. If group members perform these roles and perform them well, the facilitator's job will be easier and the group's involvement stronger. There are times, however, when a facilitator may feel that an action by a member diverts the group's attention from something that should be addressed. A compromiser, for instance, might step in too quickly to seek middle ground before all ideas have been fully explored. Thus, although these roles are considered positive, timing is important and the facilitator should pay attention to this issue.

Exhibit 7-1. Group Member Maintenance Roles

Encourager: Expresses togetherness; encourages others; gives praise

Harmonizer: Mediates and reconciles differences; suggests areas of agreement; suggests positive ways to explore differences

Compromiser: Seeks middle ground; supports both task and relationship issues; tries to find a solution that works for everyone

Gatekeeper: Asks opinions of no participants; draws people out; facilitates group interactions

Group observer: Monitors interactions; provides feedback to the group

Follower: Goes along with the group; accepts others' ideas; listens to others; supports group decisions

Source: Benne, K., & Sheats, P. (1948). Functional roles of group members. *Journal of Social Issues, 4,* 41–49.

Emergent leaders, those without official power, may emerge as leaders as group members work together (Kolb, 1999). These leaders generally perform both task and relationship functions and take the lead in moving the group forward. The emergent leadership role may be shared and may change over the course of a long-time group, depending on the skill set that is needed by the group at the time.

Identifying and Managing Dysfunctional Behaviors

We know individuals play a variety of roles, both positive and negative, in group work. Some behaviors such as continuous and inappropriate joking or a high need for attention are

116

annoying and dysfunctional. Others such as someone not doing their fair share of the work or using the group for personal purposes affect the essential nature of group functioning and may cause serious damage to group climate, process, and outcome.

The final category of roles identified by Benne and Sheats is the individual or self-centered role. These appear in Exhibit 7-2.

Exhibit 7-2. Individual Member Individual Roles

Blocker: Responds negatively to most ideas and possible solutions; raises continuous objections; returns to rejected ideas

Aggressor: Attacks the group; is critical of status of others; jokes aggressively

Dominator: Controls through superiority of tone; does not want to give up the floor; interrupts

Recognition seeker: Calls attention to self by boasting about personal achievements; brags; acts superior

Help seeker: Attempts to get sympathy from the group

Special interest pleader: Links personal ideas with those of a special interest group; expresses ideas and concerns as if speaking for the larger group

Self-confessor: Uses the group forum to express opinions that have nothing to do with the group issues or tasks

Source: Benne, K., & Sheats, P. (1948). Functional roles of group members. *Journal of Social Issues, 4,* 41–49.

Options for the facilitator. Individual, self-centered roles can be annoying, waste time, and, in general, be disruptive and detrimental to group functioning. Each of us as facilitators may at times, perhaps when we are tired or working with a group that has been challenging, overreact to certain behaviors. We need to be careful to separate the behavior from the person— in other words, to keep a positive opinion of the individual— while at the same time reduce the negative effect on the group of the behavior engaged in by the individual. Here are some suggestions on how to handle each type of disruption.

Blocker. One result of the Blocker's action is that the person receives attention. Whether this attention is the reason for the action or whether the person actually has serious issues to raise is difficult to discern when the person begins this behavior. It is only through repetitive objections and negative statements that the disruptive nature becomes more apparent. The danger is that the facilitator and the group may ignore this person when a good suggestion is made. Similar to the person who cries wolf or raises objections too often, we just don't listen attentively and therefore might miss a valid point. But, in truth, this behavior can be very draining on the group and can cause members to fall silent because they don't want their ideas criticized. Use of specific techniques that limit interaction or lead members through a step-by-step process might reduce the negative effects of this behavior. Another possible approach is to put this person in charge of something—perhaps listing comments on the board. As with all interventions, it is better to choose the lowest-level approach first. Try changes in the process that eliminate opportunity before doing anything to call attention to the Blocker.

Aggressor. This person's behavior is similar to that of the Blocker but a bit more aggressive and with a tendency to make more personal statements. Depending on the extent of these attacks, a facilitator may need to talk to the Aggressor in private if changing the process does not lessen the negativity of the statements. We all have bad days. Allowing one or two comments is one thing. If it continues, you need to consider the effect on the overall group.

Dominator. The Dominator may just like to talk. As annoying as this is, it is rarely hurtful to individuals in the group, although it is detrimental to task accomplishment. Giving the Dominator a job, as with the Blocker, sometimes works. Conversation control devices such as passing a coin as described earlier may be used for a while to make the point that each person should have a turn to speak. The facilitator may need to make rather pointed comments, such as "Does anyone else have an opinion?" or "Let's hear from someone on this side of the room" to end the monologue. The facilitator may need to break a ground rule and interrupt if the person shows no sign of winding down. Saying "Thank you, Liz, but we need to give other people a chance to give their opinions" may help. Again, specific techniques developed to reduce domination by individuals are useful for these situations.

The Recognition Seeker. This person is very similar to the Dominator and can be treated in a similar manner.

Help Seeker. This individual should be encouraged to be specific when contributing ideas to the group. Asking this person for information to clarify statements made may divert attention from the more self-serving behavior.

Special Interest Pleader. This person needs to take ownership of ideas without reverting to a group position. This person may feel that cloaking opinions within the larger context of special interests is the only way that her ideas will be acknowledged or his opinions respected. Encouraging everyone in the group to use "I" statements when expressing opinions might help. Ask, "Shawn, what experience do you have that relates to this issue?"

The Self-Confessor. This person does not acknowledge limits to self-disclosure that are observed by other group members. If the person raises very personal feelings, statements by the facilitator that the group needs to focus on task appear insensitive. Beside a loss of focus, there are other reasons why a facilitator does not want to encourage overly personal statements in a group that is not assembled for reasons of personal support. In brief, there simply is not time, and most likely not the required expertise, to process such statements. Diversion may work. Also, ask the person questions of fact when such a statement is made, or ask another question that links the statement to the discussion at hand.

Although I would hope that nothing we do as facilitators raises to the level of dysfunctional, we do all have preferences that govern how we work.

Facilitator Preferences

I remember once commenting to a friend as we were leaving a community group meeting that the tension was so thick you could cut it with a knife. My friend said, "What tension? I didn't notice any tension." Subsequent reports in the press confirmed that there was considerable discord in this group, so I probably was right about the tension, but I've always remembered the disconnect between these two interpretations of the same meeting. Most likely my interpretation was influenced by observed nonverbal communication since strident words are generally noticed and remembered by everyone present. Also, I work with groups and am used to reading a room. This means noticing facial expressions, body tension, pauses that go on too long, and eyes that don't quite make contact with someone else. If another facilitator had been with me, comparing our impressions would have been interesting.

As facilitators, we differ not only in the observations we make but in what we decide to do about them. Difficult decisions of a facilitator commonly center on when to mention tension and discord that has not been specifically expressed, when to make changes in the hope that the changes will improve the climate, and when to keep quiet and continue on with the task. What someone chooses to do or not to do depends partly on the situation (how important is climate to the task at hand—is climate getting in the way?) and partly on the experience and comfort level of the facilitator.

Task issues don't allow that luxury. A facilitator who ignores off-task behavior generally ends up with a poor outcome. Climate issues, however, lend themselves to interpretation, at

120

least in situations in which the climate is acceptable but could be improved. The same is true for relationships, which affect climate. Comparing two facilitators in similar situations, you might find one facilitator taking a quite active role in trying to build collaborative climate and improve trust and relationships and another just moving on through the task and handling only those issues that are so noticeable that they interfere with task accomplishment. An important consideration prior to any action is to check your perceptions with the group. Don't assume the group is feeling tension based solely on your observation and interpretation of nonverbal behavior.

Anytime we work with people, an understanding of our own issues and preferences will help us make decisions: what assumptions do we make about how groups should function, what group situations cause us the most difficulty, what sets us off? These issues are covered more fully in the next chapter on values and ethics and arise again in the subsequent chapter on conflict. Most facilitators do just fine with task-oriented groups that experience little in the way of interpersonal conflict, acting out, or dysfunctional behaviors. In fact, facilitators in certain types of settings may work for years and experience few of the negative situations discussed in this or subsequent chapters. Other facilitators experience discord and emotional outbursts in their facilitated groups so routinely that they view them as normal.

In any event, knowing when to react, when to intervene, and when to notice but keep quiet and see what happens comes with experience and is also, in my opinion, affected by facilitator temperament. Self-awareness is important. If you agree to accept a facilitation assignment that you know going in will involve considerable conflict, you might choose to work with a co-facilitator who is comfortable in those types of situations. This is one way to improve the odds that climate and relationship issues will be addressed. In fact, I would suggest that anyone, regardless of skill or comfort level, consider working in tandem with someone when faced with what very well might be a difficult facilitation situation. Of course, we simply don't know what will happen when we begin to facilitate a group, and a difficult situation might emerge from what should have been a routine meeting.

Summary

In this chapter, I have covered aspects of collaborative climate, group involvement and ownership, group dynamics, and group relationship and self-centered or dysfunctional roles. I ended with a discussion of facilitator preferences in handling climate and relationship issues. The next chapter focuses on values and ethical situations that arise in groups.

References

Ancona, D. G. (1990). Outward bound: Strategies for team survival in an organization. *Academy of Management Journal, 33,* 334–365.

Ancona, D. G. , & Caldwell, D. (1990). Improving the performance of new product teams. *Research Technology Management, 33*(2), 25–29.

Barnes, M. K., & Duck, S. (1994). Everyday communicative contexts for social support. In B. R. Burleson, T. L. Albrecht, & I.G. Sarason (Eds.), *Communication of social support: Messages, interactions, relationships, and community* (pp. 175–194). Thousand Oaks, CA: Sage.

Benne, K., & Sheats, P. (1948). Functional roles of group members. *Journal of Social Issues, 4,* 41–49.

Burleson, B. R., Albrecht, T. L., Goldsmith, D. J., & Sarason, I. G. (1994). Introduction: The communication of social support. In B. R. Burleson, T. L. Albrecht, & I. G. Sarason (Eds.), *Communication of social support: Messages, interactions, relationships, and community* (pp. xi-xxx). Thousand Oaks, CA: Sage.

Gibb, J. R. (1961). Defensive communication. *Journal of Communication, 11*, 141–148.

Gilley, J. W., & Boughton, N. W. (1996). *Stop managing, start coaching: How performance coaching can enhance commitment and improve productivity.* New York: McGraw-Hill.

Gilley, J. W., Morris, M. L., Waite, A. M., Coates, T., & Veliquette, A. (2010). Integrated theoretical model for building effective teams. *Advances in Developing Human Resources, 12,* 7–28.

Jones, W. H., Couch, L. L., & Scott, S. (1997). Trust and betrayal: The psychology of trust violation. In S. Briggs, R. Hogan, & J. Johnson (Eds.), *Handbook of personality* (pp. 465–482). New York: Academic Press.

Kolb, J. A. (1996). A comparison of leadership behaviors and competencies in high- and average-performance teams. *Communication Reports, 9,* 173–183.

Kolb, J. A. (1999). The effect of gender role, attitude toward leadership, and self-confidence on leader emergence: Implications for leadership development. *Human Resource Development Quarterly, 10,* 305–320.

Mayer, J. P., Davis, H. H., & Schoorman, F. D. (1995). An integrative model of organizational trust. *Academy of Management Review, 20,* 709–734.

McAllister, D. J. (1995). Affect- and cognition-based trust as foundations for interpersonal cooperation in organizations. *Academy of Management Journal, 38*(1), 24–59.

Larson, C. E., & LaFasto, C. E. (1989). *Teamwork: What must go right/what can go wrong.* Thousand Oaks, CA: Sage.

Lewis, J. D., & Weigert, A. (1985). Trust as a social reality. *Social Forces, 63,* 967–985.

Pennings, J. M., & Woiceshyn, J. (1987). A typology of organizational control and its metaphors. In S. B. Bacharach & S. M. Mitchell (Eds.), *Research in the sociology of organizations.* Greenwich, CT: JAI Press.

Scheerhorn, D., & Geist, P. (1997). Social dynamics in groups. In L. R. Frey and J. K. Barge (Eds.), *Managing group life: Communicating in decision-making groups* (pp. 81–103). Boston: Houghton Mifflin.

Thamhain, H. J., & Wilemon, D. L. (1988). Building high performing engineering project teams. In R. Katz (Ed.), *Managing professionals in innovative organizations: A collection of readings* (pp. 301–314). Cambridge, MA: Ballinger.

Whichard, J., & Kees, N. L. (2006). *Manager as facilitator.* Hartford, CT: Praeger.

Wright, J. (2005). Workplace coaching. What's it all about? *Work, 24,* 325–328.

Values and Ethics

Key Concepts

- Definitions
- Values that guide facilitation
- Ethical guidelines for decision-making groups
- Specific concerns of facilitators
- Applying values to practice

Issues related to values and ethics permeate the role of the small group facilitator. A facilitator works for and with a group and, as such, makes decisions that are in the best interest of that group. In this chapter, I discuss values that guide the facilitator role, ethical guidelines for decision-making groups, and specific ethical concerns mentioned by a group of practicing facilitators. Last, I address applying values to practice. First, what is the difference between values and ethics?

Definitions

Values may be described as guiding principles. A definition by Joseph DeVito (1976) emphasizes the relationship between attitudes, values, and behaviors, namely, "A value is an organized system of attitudes.... Values also provide us with guidelines for behavior; in effect, they direct our behavior so that it is consistent with the achievement of the values of goals we have" (p. 416). In making a distinction between values and ethics, Johannesen (1983) says that "concepts such as material success, individualism, efficiency, thrift, freedom, courage, hard work, prudence, competition, patriotism, compromise, and punctuality are all value standards that have varying degrees of potency in contemporary American culture. But we probably would not view them primarily as ethical standards of right and wrong" (p. 1). He goes on to state, however, that some value standards such as "honesty, truthfulness, fairness, and humaneness usually are used in making ethical judgments of rightness and wrongness in human behavior" (p. 1).

For our purposes in this chapter, I am defining **values** as personal beliefs or attitudes that guide our behavior and our understanding of how groups work. I have adapted a definition of ethics by Trevino and Nelson (1999) as follows: **ethical guidelines** are principles, norms, and standards of conduct governing individual group members, groups as a whole, and facilitators who work with groups.

Values that Guide Facilitation

Whether you realize it or not, you most likely have personal values that affect your conceptualization of the facilitator role. These beliefs related to how group members work together and how a facilitator works with a group form principles that guide your work. The ground rules that you choose to use (Chapters 6 and 7) reflect your values to some extent. As a starting point to thinking about your own values, consider the following values of group work identified by Auvine, Densmore, Extrom, Poole, & Shanklin (1978):

Democracy: Each person has the opportunity to partici-pate. The planning of the meeting is open and shared by the facilitator and the participants; no hierarchical organiza-tional structure functions during the session.

Responsibility: Each person is responsible for his own behavior. As a facilitator, you are responsible for what you do and how it affects the participants.

Cooperation: The facilitator and meeting participants work together to achieve collective goals.

Honesty: As a facilitator, you represent yourself and your skills honestly. You understand the limits of your skill set; you represent your feelings, concerns, and priorities hon-estly and set an expectation of honesty for others.

126

Egalitarianism: Each member has something to contribute and is given an opportunity to do so. Facilitator and participants learn from each other. Any participant has the right not to participate at any particular point.

In a different discussion of values, this one related to values that affect group work in the United States, Stech and Ratliffe (1987) list the following: democracy, individuality, openness, and loyalty. This brings up an important point about cultural differences, a topic that was discussed in Chapter 4 and elsewhere in this book. Values are affected by national culture and, to a lesser extent, by organizational and group culture. In some Asian cultures, for example, respect for elders and for people of high position would cause opinions expressed by those individuals to carry more weight than opinions voiced by others in the group.

In combining ideas from these two works, there is definite agreement on democracy as a value in groups in the United States. Both lists of values mention this. Further, the way in which Stech and Ratliffe define individuality is very close to the concept of egalitarianism as described by Auvine et al. Each individual has the right to his or her own opinion and the right to express that opinion. Openness in the latter list is similar to honesty except that Stech and Ratliffe qualify honesty by stating that "it is not workable or wise to be totally open or frank at all times" (p. 32). Loyalty, in my opinion, implies more than cooperation. Stech and Ratliffe don't mention responsibility.

In combining these lists and adding my own thoughts, I propose in Exhibit 8-1 a starting point for a list of values for facilitated groups working within the U.S. culture. You may wish to add other values that guide your work as a facilitator. Each value is explained following the list.

Exhibit 8-1. Values for U.S. Groups

❖ Democratic process
❖ Individual respect and dignity
❖ Openness
❖ Joint responsibility

Democratic process. Each person's voice is equally important. All members are equal participants in the process. All exceptions to the equality principle are noted and agreed upon. The facilitator shares power with the group and works in a consultative rather than directive manner as much as is feasible. The facilitator is transparent about choices made for group process (open, no hidden agendas).

Individual respect and dignity. All ideas and opinions are valued. Members and facilitator treat each other with respect and dignity. Individuals are allowed to "opt out" of particular activities or exercises as long as their individual choice does not disrupt the group.

Openness. Openness about issues is encouraged; personal openness is limited by context and wishes for personal privacy. Facilitator does not press members to be more open than they are willing to be. Levels of self-disclosure by both members and facilitator are appropriate for the purpose of group. Facilitators working in pure process roles share personal opinions only as related to the effective functioning of the group.

Joint responsibility. The facilitator has a responsibility to perform his/her job to the best of ability including being well prepared for the session and being neutral if in the role of process facilitator; members have responsibility to participate to the level that they are able. Both are accountable for agreed-upon goals. Facilitator has additional responsibility to be honest about experience and qualifications and to accept only those jobs that are within his or her professional capabilities.

You may think of other values that guide your work. When you work with groups that have special needs and issues, consider how your values affect the way you go about doing your job. Your values about conflict, for example, may affect the techniques you use and the extent to which you choose to intervene in conflict episodes that occur during the session.

Beyond the values that each of us holds for facilitated groups, there are other ethical considerations and guidelines that have been identified for decision-making groups.

Ethical Guidelines for Decision-Making Groups

Numerous scholars have discussed the ethical issues that arise in decision-making and problem-solving groups. Bormann (1981; 1990) urged the following eight ethical guidelines for small group discussion groups:

1. allowing making decisions without being coerced or manipulated
2. encouraging development of individual potential
3. using sound reasoning and relevant value judgments
4. avoiding conflicts focused on personal issues rather than on ideas
5. avoiding manipulating other members by selfish interest
6. being fair and accurate in presentation of information
7. communicating with each other as they would want others to communicate with them
8. using ethical criteria to judge group communication

In related research, Gouran (1990) listed five ethical responsibilities in the small group decision-making process: (1) exhibiting concern for those affected by decisions made, (2) exploring the issue with the best possible capacity, (3) avoiding misrepresentation or misuse of information, (4) protecting participants' sense of self-worth, and (5) showing respect for each other.

Again, common ground rules used by groups may reflect some of these criteria, and discussions in previous chapters have covered several of these. Protecting participants' sense of self-worth (#4, Gouran) has not been specifically discussed. What does this mean in terms of our behaviors as facilitators? Each of us may interpret this differently. Interpretations for many of us might center on treating individuals with respect and not using our power in the group in a way that would lead to member embarrassment or discomfort or cause an individual to appear in a negative light to other group members.

Often our values and beliefs regarding groups do not surface until we are faced with a certain situation in a group, or until we enter into discussions with other facilitators that allow us to compare and contrast our beliefs with those of others. If you decide to work with a cofacilitator, I suggest you have such a discussion. Otherwise, you might find yourself in the middle of a group session before realizing that you and your cofacilitator have differing views of groups and the facilitator's role. This can be a minor difference, such as your cofacilitator intervening on behavior you would overlook, or a more significant issue that involves the facilitator choosing to give personal opinion in a way that influences the group decision or outcome.

Other guidelines and criteria such as *avoiding conflicts focused on personal issues rather than on ideas* and *exploring the issue with the best possible capacity* are covered in subsequent chapters on conflict and decision-making techniques. Much of what we do in facilitating groups involves making choices. These choices have ethical ramifications for facilitators.

Specific Concerns of Facilitators

My colleagues and I (Kolb, Jin, & Song, 2009) reported data from experienced facilitators pertaining to the ethical responsibilities of facilitators. This group was a subset (20) of the facilitators who participated in development of the model presented in Chapter 3. We analyzed responses and placed them into themes or content areas. The top six themes are reported in Exhibit 8-2 in declining order of importance according to percentage of facilitators mentioning each theme. Further research is needed to explore ethical issues in more detail, but this study gives us some idea of how facilitators view their ethical responsibilities.

Exhibit 8-2. Responsibilities of Facilitators

✓ Maintaining confidentiality
✓ Establishing and sustaining professional standards for quality of process and outcome
✓ Being honest and open
✓ Remaining neutral
✓ Showing respect for people and issues
✓ Resisting pressure for predetermined outcome
Source: Kolb, J. A., Jin, S., & Song, J. (2009). Ethical responsibilities identified by small group facilitators: Implications for teamwork instruction and training. *Journal of Business and Training Education, 18,* 61–70.

Confidentiality. Under the first theme of confidentiality, mentioned by 60 percent of the facilitators, respondents described a duty to practice and model confidentiality in the hope that what was mentioned in the group would be kept within the group by all members. They were also concerned about protecting members from retaliation for their comments. These concerns are related to confidentiality about group matters, what should or should not be discussed by the facilitator with people outside the group, and what might be said to a facilitator in confidence by one group member.

Confidentiality is often mentioned as a guideline or ground rule for group functioning. Especially if the issues under discussion are sensitive, members will appreciate some assurance that what they say will be kept private. The difficulty with this, and the challenge, is that facilitators have no control over what happens outside the group. Having a ground rule of confidentiality may give members a false sense of security and lead them to say things that could be repeated and cause them some difficulties with individuals outside the group. This is my reason for not including confidentiality as a ground rule in Chapter 6. Confidentiality is important, however, and limits to confidentiality should be discussed when topics of discussion are sensitive. Group members, the facilitator, and people who have an interest in the group all need to agree in advance what limits and exceptions to confidentiality exist. The more vulnerable group members are to breaches in confidentiality, the more the facilitator should choose procedures that allow confidentiality of individual response. There is a further issue of violating rights to confidentiality of people outside the group when members raise issues in the group that outsiders might consider private.

Facilitators differ in their beliefs about the appropriateness of private communication between individual members and the facilitator. A facilitator might request that individual members each send ahead of time a list of concerns they have about an issue to be discussed at the session; the facilitator would then compile a list of all concerns and post or distribute this list at the session. This method increases the chance that all concerns will be raised without identifying an issue with a specific member, which can be important if people of differing rank or power within an organization are together in a group. A concern raised by a person with the lowest rank in the meeting might be given less attention than one raised by the boss. In this case, there is a specific reason for the private communication and all members are aware of the method of generating a list and the rationale for it. In a group that meets regularly, you might choose to raise all issues in front of the group, but in a group that meets for one or two times on a specific topic, getting all information on the table might be more important than establishing a ground rule of raising issues openly. Context is important.

A different situation arises when an individual member decides that the facilitator should be told something privately. If this information relates to a personal issue, perhaps health-related, then, of course, a facilitator should listen. An example might be someone who has a medical problem that requires attention throughout the day. Of greater concern is personal information about other individuals or the group itself that one person wants to share only with the facilitator. I once had someone "warn" me about a troublemaker in one group. This comment was made in a hallway before I even knew what was happening, but I strongly suspect that personal animosity between two people was the impetus for this remark, rather than any concern for the functioning of the group. During the session, the person labeled as a troublemaker was a pleasant, contributing member. What happened outside the room between the two people mentioned I had no way of knowing.

In another case, when I should have known better, two people asked me at break if I would raise a question with the entire group when we reconvened. It seemed an innocent enough request related to positive and negative experiences with an issue just covered. However, I could see at once when we reconvened that the question I asked caused a reaction among several people. Some turned around and looked point-edly at others. There, quite obviously, was a history here related to the issue, and I should have told the two individuals that I would give them a chance to ask the question themselves after break. It was inappropriate for me to ask a question sug-gested in private by someone else. I learned an important les-son that day about hallway conversations.

Establishing and sustaining professional standards for quality of process and outcome. Thirty-five percent of the facilitators mentioned issues categorized here. Professional standards related to everything from delivering what was promised to being genuine in one's efforts to help a group and seeking evaluations and feedback to improve facilitation skills. Much of the material found in Chapter 4 on organization and planning addresses pre-and post-work issues. An important aspect of establishing and sustaining professional standards is asking enough questions to know what is expected and then applying your expertise to planning a session or sessions that will help group members reach the designated goal. A facilitator should make process choices and decisions based on the good of the group.

Being honest and open. Thirty-five percent of the facilitators also mentioned this theme. Comments here addressed the need to model honesty in dealing with group members and maintaining transparency in decision making, which simply means being open about why you are choosing to use a particular process, procedure, or technique. A facilitator should not have a hidden agenda that would influence such decisions. Frey (2006), in related research, found that the most difficult ethical issue facilitators faced was determining "how to deal honestly and openly with what was being suggested by team members" (p. 38). Situations became more complex and sensitive when facilitators facilitated discussions pertaining to issues that members had with managers when these managers were the people who had hired the facilitators. In practice, remaining honest and open in the context of all the competing factions that may occur is a challenge. The facilitator should be honest and open about what can and cannot be shared. If the amount of closed information is sufficient to affect the facilitation, then the ethical issue may become one of whether or not the facilitator should accept the job. This theme leads directly to the next.

Remaining neutral. Thirty percent of the facilitators mentioned the theme of neutrality. Facilitators are expected to remain neutral on issues, be fair and balanced, and work for the group's interest rather than follow any personal agenda. Neutrality, as discussed in Chapter 1, is an essential element in the definition of a small group process facilitator.

Facilitators need to be aware of difficulties that might arise from a violation of the neutrality principle. The intent of neutrality is for the facilitator to have free rein in choosing interventions, techniques, and processes that will help a group move forward. The group should be able to rely on a facilitator's professional judgment in making process decisions that are appropriate for the group and the situation. If, however, a facilitator favors one outcome over another, particularly if that decision is personally beneficial, choices for process might be filtered through that lens. For example, a facilitator who favors an innovative solution might consciously or unconsciously choose a technique that encourages participants to brainstorm on a variety of options rather than a more linear technique that might move away from the innovative choice.

Facilitators may believe that they can facilitate in a professional manner even if they have opinions on the topics under consideration. Each person needs to make this decision in light of all that is known about a particular situation. Conflicts of interest should be disclosed.

Showing respect for people and issues. Fifteen percent of the facilitators mentioned this theme of respect for people, issues, and the entire process of facilitation. Comments included respecting differences among members, treating everyone with respect, not having preconceived ideas about members, and being consistently respectful and understanding of topics and people. The climate that you develop as a facilitator (Chapter 7) and the choices you make about procedures and techniques (Chapter 6) will send messages about the degree to which you respect or fail to respect the people in the room and the issues under discussion.

Resisting pressure for predetermined outcome. Fifteen percent of the facilitators also mentioned this theme. Responses here related to influence from forces outside the group and someone in charge wanting to use a facilitator to further a personal agenda. This differs from the hallway conversation matter mentioned under confidentiality because I, as the facilitator, did not realize the agenda of the two people at the time the request was made. Also, these two were not in charge of others in the room; they just wanted issues raised for reasons that were not fully disclosed. In the case of undue pressure, however, the facilitator is asked deliberately and covertly to do something to influence outcome. The facilitator may be told the desired and expected decision or outcome or may be asked to influence the group to move in a certain direction. Again, the questions that were listed in Chapter 4 should help uncover any hidden agendas at the time the facilitation is first mentioned. If your role as a facilitator is clearly defined at the onset, avoiding conflicting agendas should be easier.

Pressure is an important word here. Anyone who has worked with groups and teams in organizations realizes that at times groups are "going through the motions" when a decision may already have been made or will be made by administrators regardless of what issues or concerns are raised by groups. This happens. It is encouraging that only 15 percent of the facilitators in this study mentioned feeling external pressure to influence results. A related concern is when employees themselves believe that there is a predetermined outcome, even if a facilitator knows nothing about it and perhaps even believes that this is not the case. This belief on the part of the employees affects their willingness to participate and should be raised as an issue if a facilitator discovers this during advance planning. Whatever you do, you want to be as transparent as possible when working with a group. Failure to do so not only has ethical implications but will quickly reduce your effectiveness.

It may have crossed your mind that the less you know, the less likely you are to have an ethical dilemma or conflict. If you don't ask many questions, you won't know about external factors and constraints and will be free to work with the group. This comment comes up in discussions of facilitation. Situations vary, but I can't think of any case in which failure to know pertinent information would be a good choice. At times, you are asked to come in with very little advance notice and you have no chance to ask questions other than the basics of Who? What? When? and Where? At other times, when you begin to feel uneasy about what is being presented to you, you might ask yourself this question: Am I being asked to keep information from the group? If the answer is yes, you may have a problem or dilemma that needs to be resolved. Involvement in discussions of potential ethical issues might help facilitators know what to expect and be better prepared to handle such situations.

Applying Values to Practice

Heightened awareness of ethical issues has been reported in participants who completed training in which they were exposed to a variety of ethical situations through the use of short scenarios and vignettes (Frisque & Kolb, 2008). Just thinking about issues that might happen is good preparation for times in which we need to make decisions about what is the ethical thing to do. The use of hypothetical situations is used frequently by people in a variety of fields and occupations as a tool to improve both awareness of and ability to deal with ethical situations that arise in the workplace (Frisque, Lin, & Kolb, 2004; Moon & Woolliams, 2000; Sanyal, 1999). People in an ethical dilemma often think that they have only one or two options. Upon reflection, they may discover options or choices that were not readily apparent. With this in mind, I present two scenarios below. In reading them, instead of deciding immediately what you would do, ask yourself the following questions:

Exhibit 8-3. Ethical Considerations

❖ What are the issues involved?

❖ How do the ethical issues and group work values discussed in this chapter affect this scenario?

❖ What are my options?

❖ What are the ramifications or results of each option?

❖ What would I do?

Scenario 1: During a rather routine meeting of a group that has been in existence for six months, Kate, one of the members, came in late just as the group was completing a break. She came directly from a meeting with her boss and was obviously quite excited. Another member, Carol, who works in Kate's department, asks her what happened. Kate quickly began giving details on what was obviously an important conversation involving details that the boss probably did not intend to become a topic of group discussion. As soon as she took a breath, you brought the group back to the issue they had been discussing before break.

Scenario 2: David, one of the members of a long standing project group, is acting in a way that is out of character for him. He became very upset at a fairly benign comment made by another member, Jack, and made a sarcastic and rather hurtful comment to Marilyn, a recent addition to the group who does not really know the others very well. After that, David sat in silence. As soon as break was called, he rushed from the room. During break, you overhead Jack apologizing for David to Marilyn and saying that David is having some personal problems and might be drinking more than usual.

Discussion of scenarios. Think through each of these situations and consider what you would do before you read this section.

Scenario 1 has to do with issues of confidentiality and professional standards and the value of openness. Kate has offered information to the group on issues that don't affect group members, although Carol has the same boss and they all work for the same company. Group members might mention something that will get back to her boss and get Kate in trouble. You are also concerned that the group now has information that Kate's boss may consider confidential.

Your options include—do nothing, raise the issue of confidentiality with the group without speaking to Kate first, raise the issue with the group after break and after speaking with Kate, speak only to Kate privately after the group session, speak with Kate and Carol after the group session, ask Kate to mention to her boss that she talked about what was said in the meeting, talk to her boss yourself and say that some private information was inadvertently disclosed in group meeting, a combination of these actions, some other choice.

Ideally, of course, you want no harm to come to Kate, to any group member, to Kate's boss, or to the company because of confidential information that was disclosed during the group. If you had acted more quickly, perhaps you could have suggested to Kate that she talk with Carol later. There is a chance that once she calmed down a bit, she would have edited what she said. But, it is too late to rewind the tape and erase her disclosure. So now what? Saying nothing at all to the group increases the chance that the disclosure will be repeated. Saying something to the boss or asking Kate to tell the boss about her disclosure at the meeting puts Kate at a possible disadvantage. Not informing the boss puts the boss at a disadvantage and may have some repercussions for the department and company. What action(s) do you choose?

139

Scenario 2. Values of respect and openness are relevant here as are the issues of confidentiality, professional responsibility, respect for others, and joint responsibility. Since David left right away, you have no option to talk with him privately unless you seek him out after the group session. He may be seriously depressed and need some help. If he is drinking on the job, you most likely have a responsibility to report this, but you don't know for a fact that he was drinking. That was Jack's opinion. Marilyn plus other group members may be feeling upset about what happened. Your options include doing nothing, contacting David to discuss his behavior in the group, speaking with Marilyn privately to explain that today's behavior was unusual, speaking with the entire group in a general way about people saying things that hurt others and the effect of that behavior, speaking with Jack after the group session to get more information, speaking with someone in Human Resources who is designated to handle such employee situations, doing nothing, a combination of these actions, another choice. A primary concern here is what responsibility do you have toward David? What can you do without violating his personal privacy? Do you consider his behavior serious enough that you should speak with him or someone else? Or, is this none of your concern? What would you do?

If you were actually in these situations, you would have more information or, at the very least, a context for what happened. Your actual decision in these two cases is less relevant for our purposes here than the thought processes that brought you to your decision. Anyone who works closely with people, and facilitators certainly fit that description, will face issues and challenges that may be difficult to resolve. There may not be a clear-cut solution. Every option has ramifications and only by weighing those options can we decide what to do. When we are faced with a situation, we may have seconds to decide what to do. A consideration of values is helpful in giving each of us some advance preparation time that will help us decide on appropriate actions.

Summary

In this chapter, I discussed values that guide the facilitator role, ethical guidelines for decision-making groups, specific ethical concerns mentioned by a group of practicing facilitators, and the application of values to how we perform our job as facilitators. We turn next to conflict. How we choose to handle conflict in groups is a reflection of our opinion on the importance of conflict—or to say this another way, the values we hold about conflicts in groups.

References

Auvine, B., Densmore, B., Extrom, M., Poole, S., & Shanklin, M. (1978). *A manual for group facilitators*. Madison, WI: The Center for Conflict Resolution.

Bormann, E. G. (1981). Ethical standards for interpersonal/ small group communication. *Communication 6(2)*, 267–286.

Bormann, E. G. (1990). *Small group communication: Theory and practice* (3rd ed.). New York: Harper & Row.

DeVito, J. A. (1976). *The interpersonal communication book*. New York: Harper & Row.

Frey, L. R. (2006). Introduction: Facilitating group communication in context. L. R. Frey (Ed.), *Facilitating group communication in context: Innovations and applications with natural groups* (pp. 1–59). Cresskill, NJ: Hampton Press.

Frisque, D. A., & Kolb, J. A. (2008). The effects of an ethics training program on attitude, knowledge, and transfer of training of office professionals: A treatment- and control- group design. *Human Resource Development Quarterly, 19*, 35–53.

Frisque, D. A., Lin, H., & Kolb, J. A. (2004). Preparing professionals to face ethical challenges in today's workplace: Review of the literature, implications for PI, and a proposed research agenda. *Performance Improvement Quarterly, 17*(2), 28–45.

Gouran, D. (1990). *Making decisions in groups: Choices and consequences.* Prospect Heights, IL: Waveland.

Johannesen, R. L. (1983). *Ethics in human communication* (2nd ed.). Prospect Heights, IL: Waveland.

Kolb, J. A., Jin, S., & Song, J. (2009). Ethical responsibilities identified by small group facilitators: Implications for teamwork instruction and training. *Journal of Business and Training Education, 18,* 61–70.

Moon, C. J., & Woolliams, P. (2000). Managing cross cultural business ethics. *Journal of Business Ethics, 27,* 105–115.

Sanyal, R. N. (1999). An experiential approach to teaching ethics in international business. *Teaching Business Ethics, 4,* 137–149.

Stech, E., & Ratliffe, S. A. (1987). *Effective group communication: How to get action by working in groups.* Lincolnwood, IL: National Textbook Company.

Trevino, L. K., & Nelson, K. A. (1999). *Managing business ethics: Straight talk about learning to do it right.* New York: John Wiley & Sons.

Conflict

Key Concepts

- Nature of conflict
- Importance of climate and ground rules
- Types of conflict
- Focusing on interests, not positions
- Avoiding groupthink
- Values about conflict

A previous discussion about relationships and climate provides important background for this chapter. Conflict: how it emerges, whether it is valued or discouraged, and ways in which it is managed all affect and are affected by climate. In this chapter, I talk first about the nature of conflict; then discuss the importance of climate and ground rules; the types of conflict, both issue-based and personal, that might occur; the value in focusing on interests rather than positions "for" or "against" an issue; and behaviors to look for in our quest to avoid groupthink. I end with some thoughts about how facilitators choose to handle conflict.

Nature of Conflict

Although the word "conflict" often has a negative connotation, disagreement among group members on issues can improve a group's decision making and is generally viewed as a positive influence. Conflict is, by nature, interactive. This interactive nature results in a cycle of initiation-response-counterresponse (Folger & Poole, 1984). Communication plays a central role in this cycle in three ways:

- Communication behavior often *creates* conflict.
- Communication behavior *reflects* conflict.

- Communication is the *vehicle* for the productive or destructive management of conflict (Hocker & Wilmot, 1991, p. 13).

In groups, conflict over issues is positive if handled in a productive way and generally means that members are paying attention and invested in the outcome. Conflicts of a personal nature, however, can drain energy from a group and result in a loss of focus. An important job of a facilitator is to model and manage communication within the group in a way that encourages the expression of differences of opinion over group issues and procedural matters and discourages conflicts during group time over personal issues that are not relevant to the task at hand.

An interpersonal conflict involving only two members may resonate throughout the group and affect the relationships among all group members as each member forms an opinion and perhaps makes a judgment about the conflict and the participants. In long-term groups, the facilitator needs to find a way to allow members to work out personal disagreements. In short-term groups, however, the necessity to focus on task accomplishment in the limited time available precludes spending much time on interpersonal conflicts that are not task related. Separating issue-based comments from personal ones is one way to encourage productive disagreement. An example may help make this point.

If a group member, John, says, "I don't agree with what we're doing here. I don't like the approach we're taking," he raises an issue that needs to be addressed since it involves the group task. If William responds by saying, "Don't listen to John; he always complains," this is, again, an issue for the group even though it involves a personal statement toward John by William. That personal statement needs to be addressed by the facilitator as in the following dialogue:

Facilitator: William, remember our ground rule to criticize ideas, not people. John, please tell us the reasons why you don't like this approach.

(John gives his reasons. The facilitator probes for factual information instead of opinion.)

Facilitator: What do the rest of you think about the concerns John raised?

If, however, John replies to William with a personal derogatory comment and William responds in kind, the interpersonal conflict between these two group members has moved beyond the task at hand. The facilitator would focus on whatever John has to say about the approach being used and, in a short-term group, might ask the two members to continue their personal exchange outside the group. There are differences in opinion on the extent to which personal conflict should be handled within a group, and I will return to this later in the chapter. The interactive nature of conflict can result in a statement-response-statement sequence that quickly spirals out of control.

Folger and Poole (1984) provide a summary of four guiding principles in conflict interaction that are useful to this discussion:

1. Patterns of behavior in conflicts tend to perpetuate themselves.

2. As senseless and chaotic as conflict interaction may appear, it has a general direction that can be understood.

3. Conflict interaction is sustained by the moves and countermoves of participants; moves and countermoves are based on the power participants exert.

4. Conflict interaction affects the relationship between participants (p. 44).

Power, as used by Folger and Poole, is meant in a positive sense as the capacity to act effectively. In that sense, someone who acts effectively may be able to influence others to adapt his or her point of view. The amount of power someone is willing to employ may determine the outcome of a conflict situation.

A facilitator can choose an approach that helps mitigate individual power and encourages an exploration of all ideas. Likewise, climate, especially in a long standing group, has an effect on the types of conflicts that are likely to emerge, the respect given to ideas and concerns expressed by all members, and the ways in which conflicts are resolved.

Importance of Climate and Ground Rules

Climate and conflict have a reciprocal relationship; each affects the other. Group climate emerges from and builds upon the interactions and relationships among members. Norms of behavior that exist in long standing groups have an effect on the ways in which disagreements are handled. And the ways in which disagreements are handled over time have an effect on climate. In short-term groups, lack of history makes facilitator action and the use of supportive communication and appropriate ground rules even more important.

Ground rules for productive conflict. Supportive behaviors, first described in a discussion of climate in Chapter 7, include describing without judgment, focusing on problem orientation and emphasizing mutual interests, being open and honest, conveying empathy and concern, valuing others and their ideas, and seeking and considering other points of view (Gibb, 1961). These behaviors serve to create a climate that encourages open discussion of varying points of view. These supportive behaviors have some overlap with ground rules discussed in Chapter 6. I've combined both in the list in Exhibit 9-1.

146

Exhibit 9-1. Ground Rules for
Conflict Resolution

1. Focus on the problem.
2. Identify mutual interests.
3. Encourage open discussion of all points of view.
4. Use descriptive, not judging, language.
5. Criticize ideas, not people.
6. Avoid nonverbal communication that disrespects an idea or person.
7. Separate fact from opinion.
8. Verify all information
9. Agree on the meaning of words and terms.
10. Focus on interests, not positions.

A reminder, and perhaps a posting, of ground rules and a discussion with members of any additional ground rules that might be needed are important steps when beginning a discussion that involves substantial difference of opinion. If you are using a specific approach, ground rules may be imbedded in that process. In that case, I suggest a brief reminder of only two ground rules: "criticize ideas not people" and "avoid nonverbal communication that disrespects an idea or person." In conflict situations, much meaning can be conveyed by eye rolls, sighs, body language, and sarcasm. To the extent possible, you want to encourage supportive, productive use of verbal and nonverbal communication.

Voicing dissent appropriately. A group norm of "criticize ideas, not people" should help establish the behavior of voicing differences of opinion in a respectful way. If questions asked before the facilitation (Chapter 4) uncover issues that almost certainly will be sensitive for the group, a forward-thinking facilitator will consider that conflict might very well be a part of the session and will plan, set ground rules, and choose an approach accordingly. However, conflicts, even heated conflicts, can bubble up in unexpected ways and over issues that do not appear on the surface to be ones that should create disagreement or dissent. Remember our earlier discussion of "It's not what you say, it's how you say it." A norm of expressing disagreement with issues and procedures in a way that explains points of concern without disrespecting individuals is one that generally exists in long-term groups. In one-time or short-term groups, however, you don't have that history and need to rely on ground rules and member agreement on what is and is not acceptable discourse.

Use of devil's advocate. The "devil's advocate" role of voicing negative aspects of an issue is one that many may recognize. Group members may even open a comment by saying, "If I may play devil's advocate for a while...." Freedom to raise objections and voice concerns is a positive norm for a group. As a facilitator, you can encourage dissent by the type of questions you ask. If all the issues raised by a group have been positive, you might ask, "What are some negative issues? Negative ramifications?" Few decisions are so clear cut that nothing at all negative might emerge. Also, a facilitator asking members to consider negative issues provides a framework for raising dissent. Many of the techniques covered in subsequent chapters have steps that include consideration of positives and negatives for each decision option.

Verifying information and clarifying terms. Ground rules 8 and 9 stated earlier deserve further exploration. As was discussed in Chapter 2, groups try to make decisions even when information is insufficient. As frustrating as that is, a worse scenario occurs when group members have erroneous information that is then used as the basis for decision making. This information may take the form of unsubstantiated rumors. Before moving forward, a group needs to be sure that information being used is accurate. More information may be requested before a decision is made, as in the facilitator account presented later in this chapter. In that case, experts were brought in to provide missing information so that group members could have a full understanding of issues involved. Another common problem is in the varying definitions people use for terms. Although it simplifies conflict too much to say that language can lead to misunderstandings that then lead to conflict, it is important to check that people agree on the meaning of terms and phrases that are used in a discussion. Don't waste the group's energy in circular discussions that could easily be resolved with clarification of terms.

Being proactive. Facilitators in research reported by Kolb and Rothwell (2000) often stated that they wished they had taken some action before conflict escalated. Waiting and hoping things get better is rarely a good idea. Choose your approach carefully, remind participants of group norms, particularly in relation to voicing criticism, and "take the pulse" of the group as the discussion moves forward. As facilitators, we want issue-based conflict to occur since this generally means that people are invested in the outcome and paying attention. What we don't want is personality-based, nonconstructive conflict. Unfortunately, both types occur in groups.

Types of Conflict

Putnam (1986) uses the terms "substantive," "procedural," and "affective" to describe types of conflicts. Substantive conflicts involve disagreements over members' ideas and group issues. Procedural conflict is disagreement among group members about the methods of process that should be followed by the group in accomplishing a goal. Affective conflicts involve people's feelings and the way members relate to each other. Since both substantive and procedure conflicts are task related, I will combine those two for our purposes in discussing conflicts in groups.

Substantive/procedural conflict. Differences of opinion about task issues (substantive/procedural conflicts) are considered healthy and can lead to improved performance. One example from facilitator accounts on managing conflicts reported by Kolb and Rothwell (1999) is relevant here and has been modified slightly:

> A group came together to plan a specific training program but could not agree on an approach. After some arguments back and forth, the facilitator called for a break and then reconvened, summarized the concerns raised, and asked questions to clarify the primary issues. Experts were brought in to provide additional information. The result was that members reached a better understanding of each other's concerns and were able to move forward. A portion of the facilitator's comments in reflecting on this situation is as follows, "I tend to try to solve problems before I know the root cause. I believe if I ask questions & let the group talk I will more likely be able to steer the group to a win-win" (p. 514).

The phrase "win-win" (Jandt & Gillette, 1985) is commonly used in business and elsewhere when the intent is to find a solution that works for everyone. This is an approach that might be used when a focus on the issues involved seems warranted. In the example above, the issue being discussed was relevant to the purpose of the group and involved all members. The next type of conflict is not relevant to the group task and involves, directly at least, only a few members. Such conflicts are labeled affective or interpersonal.

Affective/interpersonal conflict. Affective conflicts involve people's feelings and the way in which members relate to each other. Although conflicts over substantive issues may also involve people's feelings, interpersonal conflict is about feelings and relationships above all and, as we are considering such conflict, is not connected in any essential way to group issues or tasks. Such conflicts may prevent the group from accomplishing its purpose if group time and energy become invested in these interpersonal, oftentimes emotional, battles. An example modified from Kolb and Rothwell (1999) follows:

> A personal conflict arose between some group participants. The facilitator called a break for the group and then handled the problem in a private setting with the individuals involved. Conflict was eliminated in the session but further private sessions were needed to solve their problems. The facilitator in reflections indicated that this choice was one s/he would make again and did not think involving the entire group was a good idea.

How to handle? Substantive conflicts are important to both task and relationship and improve the functioning and outcomes of the group. Most facilitators would agree that addressing and resolving substantive issues is a good use of group time. Interpersonal conflicts are a different story. Such disagreements between individuals can very well have a negative effect on group functioning. But whether or not group members and group time should be used to discuss and resolve these conflicts is a decision that needs to be made by the facilitator and, in some cases, the group. Factors to be considered include the purpose of the group (specifically whether one of the purposes of the group is to improve its process), the skills of group members, time available, size of the group, and the skills of the facilitator. In short-term facilitated sessions in organizational contexts, facilitators may make the decision to handle these situations privately with the people involved, as was the case in the example just cited.

Facilitator attempts to resolve such conflicts are sometimes called maintenance process interventions (Reddy, 1994) or deeper-level interventions (Schwarz, 1994). In discussing personal conflicts that occur between individuals in groups that have improvement of group process as a goal, Schwarz (1994) might involve group members by asking such questions as "How do you feel toward Joe and Bob when this happens?" and "Bob, why do you think you end up in conflicts more frequently than other group members?" (p. 113). Involving the entire group in discussions of conflicts that occur between two group members works well when the group is more relationship than task focused and when the purpose or one of the purposes of the group is to improve process. For other short-term or more task-oriented groups, delving into emotional areas may be beyond the scope of the organizational facilitation situation and the skills of group members and the facilitator.

Knowing the context is particularly important in choosing how to handle personal conflicts among individuals. How well does the facilitator know the people in the group, how well do members know each other, how large is the group, how intense is the conflict: all are factors that influence facilitator options. If you know the group well and two people are just starting to quarrel on a personal issue, stating that the group needs to stay on topic and asking whether anything they're raising has implications for the group might be enough to stop the personal comments or put them on hold.

Calling a break, as was mentioned by the facilitator in the second example given earlier, is a popular choice among facilitators. Of course, you can't have that as your only tool or groups would be spending hours in break time. Well used, however, breaks can provide a short time to calm down, reflect, and regroup. They also allow the facilitator time to talk briefly with individual group members. The important thing to keep in mind is that you can't, usually, just ignore personal conflicts. Nor can you invest substantial group time and energy on them. We now return to substantive conflict—conflict about issues that are directly relevant to the group's task and functioning—and an approach that is based on a focus on interests rather than positions.

Focusing on Interests Rather than Positions

An approach labeled *win-win* and used by the facilitator in the first example cited in this chapter is also referred to as a focus on interests over positions. Both describe attempts to find solutions that are agreeable to everyone. The purpose is to move people away from positions of "for" or "against" a certain issue or plan of action and toward an examination of the interests or reasons why they hold a certain position. A focus on interests does not mean that all persons in a conflict or difference of opinion can get everything they want. It does mean that people attempt to come to an accommodation that considers issues raised by everyone. The goal is to avoid a decision of "this side wins, the other side loses." Instead of a "fixed pie" in which each person's portion is determined by the portion size given to others, perhaps group members can find a way to expand the pie. A solution previously unconsidered may emerge as satisfactory to everyone.

One approach to use with a group that has two or more positions that seem to be in conflict with each other is to unpack the positions and interests as indicated in Exhibit 9-2.

Exhibit 9-2. Interest-Based Approach to Conflict

❖ Begin with a statement that presents each position.

❖ Identify the interests behind each position.

❖ Allow each side time to explain their views.

❖ Ask each side to restate the views and concerns of the other.

❖ Check for thorough understanding of interests.

❖ Search for areas of agreement.

❖ Clarify disagreements.

❖ Brainstorm options that address all interests.

❖ Check for consensus or desired outcome.

You need to be realistic in determining the level of agreement that is possible. Depending on the situation, you may not be able to reach a decision that satisfies everyone. Some people avoid the term *win-win* for this reason, believing that it creates unrealistic expectations. Also, consensus may not be the most desirable outcome. A consensus decision that becomes watered down in the process of reaching agreement may end up being of little value. A better outcome might be a decision that is approved by a majority or one that all members can live with. You should decide before discussions begin what level of agreement is desired. The more important the decision, the more time and effort that should be expended on reaching consensus.

Even if conflict does not rise to the level of people having set positions *for* or *against*, raising concerns and possible negative ramifications of a decision should be encouraged. By unpacking the positions and concerns voiced by group members, you uncover underlying issues and interests. Usually, members will find some areas of agreement that can be used to build workable options and solutions. The necessity of raising potential negative issues before finalizing a decision is a lesson learned that has been described as groupthink.

Avoiding Groupthink

Another term almost as popular as *win-win* is *groupthink*. Janis's (1971; 1983) often-cited work on groupthink found that highly cohesive groups suspend critical thinking and adopt proposed solutions too quickly. Harmony among group members becomes more important than a critical examination of issues. This absence of productive conflict over issues can cause a group to make a decision that, upon further reflection, would have been considered ill advised. In his early work, Janis spent two years examining group decision making in the political policy-making arena such as the discussions leading to the Bay of Pigs invasion during the administration of President John Kennedy. He noted that people involved in all the decisions he studied were extremely talented and well versed in the issues involved. He wondered why, then, were points of disagreement not raised? This led him to a closer examination of the dangers of highly cohesive groups and the conclusion that too much cohesion can work against effective group functioning. He noticed that instead of cohesiveness among group members leading to a greater expression of dissent, which might be expected as members become more comfortable with one another, the opposite happened. Members began believing that their misgivings were not relevant and hesitated to voice them, not wanting to detract from feelings of group cohesion and consensus.

Some symptoms (in bold type) and examples of comments that might occur from groupthink adapted from Janis (1971) are taken from Albanese, Franklin, and Wright (1997, p. 505):

Pressure on those who deviate from majority opinion:

"Oh, I'm sure he/she does not mean to differ from the position the rest of us are taking."

Fearing results of deviating from majority opinion:

"I'd better not express my viewpoint because I just might alienate the rest of the group."

Illusion of consensus and unanimity:

"Well, I guess we all are in total agreement on going ahead with this project."

Unquestioned belief in group's morality:

"We've always done the right thing. Our 'in' reputation is solid. Let's go ahead."

Channeling out negative feedback:

"Sure, that's contrary to the view we're taking, but consider the source."

As facilitators, we are pleased when a collaborative climate develops in a group. And we have a right to feel a sense of accomplishment since this climate derives at least partially from the ground rules, positive interactions, working relation-ships, and functional processes encouraged by a facilitator. We need to be alert, however, to the danger of too much cohesion. If we hear comments such as the ones above expressed by group members, this is a signal that we should perhaps focus members' attention on negative aspects of a decision or solution.

If just the thought of a conflict erupting in your facilitated session causes you to become incredibly tense, you might want to consider your personal values related to conflict.

Personal Values about Conflict

A facilitator's personal views and comfort level with conflict might affect the climate of the group, techniques used for deci-sion making and problem solving, and the way in which the facilitator chooses to handle or even acknowledge conflict within a group. As one example, a facilitator who is very uncomfortable with conflict of any kind might keep the group from fully discussing substantive issues that are essential for the group's success by intervening at the first sign of disagree-ment and changing the direction of the discussion. Assuming the group allows this misdirection, the decisions made by that group may very well suffer because negative issues were not allowed to surface. Alternatively, a facilitator who enjoys "stir-ring things up" might encourage a level of conflict that is inap-propriate given the purpose and culture of the group.

The list of questions in Exhibit 9-3 will give you an idea of how you currently handle conflict in your facilitated groups. Knowing our sensitivity to conflict is one way to keep our own attitudes from affecting our ability to facilitate groups in conflict.

Exhibit 9-3. How I Handle Conflicts in Groups

❖ I view conflict over issues as a chance to improve decisions.

❖ I choose techniques that explore both positive and negative aspects of an issue.

❖ I use ground rules such as *criticize issues, not people.*

❖ I believe that I am able to successfully handle personal conflicts that arise between members.

❖ I am able to read a room and sense discomfort.

❖ I explore reasons for discomfort when answers seem important to the task and group.

❖ I have a good sense of when to probe and when to move on.

❖ I don't stir things up for no reason.

If you've answered "yes" to most of these questions, then, assuming your self-perception accurately reflects your behaviors—a big assumption by the way—you should be able to handle the conflicts that arise in most groups. Whatever your personal feelings and values regarding conflict, you acknowledge the positive value of conflicts in groups and encourage groups to handle disagreements in a way that will benefit the group.

If you did not answer "yes" to very many of these questions, you aren't alone. Facilitators in a study reported by Kolb and Rothwell (2000) identified handling internal conflict in groups as their primary challenge. If you feel uncomfortable when conflict arises, you might want to consider working with a co-facilitator in situations in which you know conflict will emerge. In long-term groups, you could encourage group members to develop norms that encourage positive dissent. The devil's advocate role, for example, can rotate among members until everyone gets into the habit of raising negative issues that may impact a decision. Several of the decision-making problem-solving techniques covered in later chapters have steps that take groups through an orderly process of examining pros and cons. Conflict cannot and should not be avoided, but it can be handled thoughtfully.

Summary

In this chapter, I discussed the nature of conflict and the importance of climate and ground rules. I then described the types of conflict, both issue-based and personal, that might occur; approaches to handling issue-based conflict; and the negative groupthink aspect that might come from too much cohesion. I ended with some thoughts about how a facilitator chooses to handle conflict. Our next chapter focuses on creativity. I've seen "Avoid Groupthink" signs posted in creative offices, which shows how creativity and conflict both benefit from an exploration of all facets of an issue or problem.

References

Albanese, R., Franklin, G. M., & Wright, P. (1997). *Management* (rev. ed.). Houston, TX: Dame Publications.

Folger, J. P., & Poole, M. S. (1984). *Working through conflict: A communication perspective.* Dallas, TX: Scott Foresman and Company.

Gibb, J. R. (1961). Defensive communication. *Journal of Communication, 11,* 141–148.

Hocker, J. L., & Wilmot, W. W. (1991). *Interpersonal conflict* (3rd ed.). Dubuque, IA: William C. Brown.

Jandt, F. E. , & Gillette, P. (1985). *Win-win negotiating: Turning conflict into agreement.* New York: John Wiley & Sons.

Janis, I. (1971). Groupthink among policy makers. In N. Sanford & C. Cornstock & Associates (Eds.), *Sanctions for evil.* San Francisco, CA: Jossey-Bass.

Janis, I. (1983). *Groupthink. Psychological studies of policy decisions and fiascoes* (2nd ed.). Boston: Houghton Mifflin.

Kolb, J. A., & Rothwell, W. J. (1999). Conflicts that arise in small group facilitation: A descriptive study of accounts, actions, outcomes, and assessments. In R. J. Torraco (Ed.), *1999 Conference Proceedings of the Academy of Human Resource Development* (pp. 512–519). Baton Rouge, LA: The Academy of Human Resource Development.

Kolb, J. A., & Rothwell, W. J. (2000). Challenges and problems reported by small group facilitators. *Performance Improvement Quarterly, 13*(4), 122–136.

Putnam, L. L. (1986). Conflict in group decision-making. In R. Y. Hirokawa & M. S. Poole (Eds.), *Communication and group decision-making* (pp. 175–196). Beverly Hills, CA: Sage.

Reddy, W. B. (1994). *Intervention skills: Process consultation for small groups and teams.* San Diego, CA: Pfeiffer & Company.

Schwarz, R. M. (1994*). The skilled facilitator: Practical wisdom for developing effective groups.* San Francisco, CA: Jossey-Bass.

 **Creativity**

Key Concepts

- What is creativity?
- Suggestions for creative problem solving
- Stimulating creativity in groups
- Importance of work environment and trust
- Strategies to stimulate creativity

Creative solutions are needed in our current climate—problems are increasingly complex yet resources are limited. Two common phrases today are "Do more with less" and "Think outside the box." To do either requires creativity. Since considerable problem solving occurs in group settings, this chapter explores the process of creative problem solving, ways in which creativity can be encouraged, and strategies to use to stimulate creativity.

What Is Creativity?

Davis (1983) describes the creative process as "combining or perceiving relationships of previously unrelated ideas" (p. 6). Intuition, too, is discussed in terms of relationships among ideas or patterns; these patterns consist of clusters of knowledge acquired by long experience that allow people to make judgments (Simon, 1987). What we call intuition, according to Simon, is information stored in chunks and patterns in long-term memory. During creative or lateral thinking (DeBono, 1968), old patterns are reassembled as a result of experience and revelation in a new way. Steiner (1988), in describing the creative process, says that "up to a point, it may be hard to distinguish from totally non-productive behavior: undisciplined disorder, aimless rambling, even total activity" (p. 206). He lists the following three characteristics:

1. **Irregular process.** "Creativity is rarely a matter of gradual, step-by-step progress; it is more often a pattern of large and largely unpredictable leaps after relatively long periods of no apparent progress" (p. 206).

2. **Suspended judgment.** The creative process "often requires and exhibits suspended judgment" (p. 206) and he warns of the dangers of early commitment to one strategy or decision.

3. **Undisciplined exploration.** Undisciplined thinking in early stages expands the options that will be considered.

These "large and largely unpredictable leaps"—fueled by intuition, new discovery, or likely a combination of both—form the basis of the creative process. Even though the process is undisciplined, there are ways to foster creativity.

Creative Problem Solving

The following suggestions for creative problem solving are offered by Shapero (1988):

1. Soak yourself in the problem. Look at every aspect. Read, talk to people, question premises. Don't accept that it cannot be solved.

2. Play with the problem. Stay loose and flexible. Turn the problem inside out and approach from different directions. Change different aspects of the problem.

3. Suspend judgment. Fight any tendency to find an early solution. Suspend judgment. If solutions come up, write them down but put aside until later.

4. Come up with a minimum of two solutions. Shapero cites research from Hyman and Anderson (1965) that "asking people for two solutions, as compared to one, increased the number of 'creative' solutions from 16 percent to 52 percent" (p. 219). There was also an

increase of 25 percent when people were asked for three solutions but not all responded.

5. When stuck, try something else or take a break. Try a different way of picturing the problem and solution. Go from words to pictures. Take a break. Let your subconscious work.

Stimulating Creativity in Groups

Keeping this definition and these suggestions in mind, what can facilitators do to stimulate creativity in group sessions?

Give ideas time to incubate. As was discussed in Chapter 4, a division of tasks, completing some work before and after a face-to-face session, can be very productive. Participants might be asked to consider all aspects of a problem and bring some off-the-wall ideas to the group meeting. Having time between stages of a process also is useful since this allows "ideas to incubate" (Sisk & Williams, 1981, p. 120). If during pre-planning, you learn that a full day has been set aside for a creative work session, you could mention that two half-day sessions might be more conducive to a generation of creative solutions.

Use brief creativity exercises. What I sometimes do before beginning problem-solving, or whenever a group needs a mental break, is hold up a pencil, coffee mug, or marker and give members two minutes to write down all the uses in addition to the traditional one for the object. In a small group, I ask them to do this individually. In a larger group that has members sitting together at small tables, members work individually and then with people at their tables to come up with a table total. At the end of two minutes, a show of hands will determine who has 20 ideas, 30, and so on. The winning individual or group reads the list of ideas, and other people in the room can challenge any item and add ideas they had that were not listed. There may or may not be some small prize or prizes for the winners, perhaps pencils or some token. This exercise is short and can be used in a variety of ways—primarily it makes a point about the value of seeing things differently. I've always found that groups enjoy it.

Ask "Why not?" Establish a group norm that encourages group members to ask "Why not?" when someone says something cannot be done. Probe for assumptions and faulty data. Ask individuals to explore ideas as if there were no limitations. Instead of accepting "it can't be done" as a fact, ask for reasons behind the statement and see if creative thinking can come up with a way to move forward.

Challenge assumptions. Listen closely to determine what assumptions are being made. Assumptions aren't always valid, but they almost always limit options. Here's an example from a class I took as a graduate student. The instructor told us that we would each be given a picture to copy. My first thought was, "I can't draw." When the picture was given to me, however, it was reversed (bottom side up) so that I saw no discernable form, just a series of lines. I copied what I saw. When I finished and turned both my copy and the original picture right side up, my drawing looked very much like the picture of a man reading a newspaper. We all held up our drawings, and they all looked very much like the original picture. The point of the exercise was that expectations were low—what we were copying seemed abstract and meaningless. Assumptions, especially those that relate to what we can or cannot do or what is or is not viewed as realistic, limit performance. In a group, faulty assumptions can keep a group from exploring an option that might be a viable solution to a problem.

Use visuals or other alternatives to words. Ask members to display the problem in pictures or in some abstract fashion. Or draw a segment of a fence on the board. Ask what options are available when you come to a fence: jump over, tunnel under, go around. What else? What if the fence is circular? Did the group make the assumption that the fence went in a straight line?

What other incorrect assumptions might they be making? You might also show a very brief portion of a picture that looks like one thing but actually is something else. You could have the same discussion about making assumptions that limit thinking.

Open mind locks. Mind locks are assumptions about how people should be or act. They close the mind. Lumsden and Lumsden (1993) list the following mind locks originally identified by Roger von Oech in 1983.

1. The right answer.
2. That's not logical.
3. Follow the rules.
4. Be practical.
5. Avoid ambiguity.
6. To err is wrong.
7. Play is frivolous.
8. That's not my area.
9. Don't be foolish.
10. I'm not creative (pp. 149–150).

These statements all limit creativity. Mind lock #5 says, "Avoid ambiguity." I would go a step further and say "celebrate" ambiguity.

Celebrate ambiguity. In my own research on teams (Kolb, 1996), I found that scores on a measurement of tolerance for uncertainty (ambiguity) were higher for leaders of high-performing teams than for leaders of average-performing teams. This tolerance is especially important in creative teams. Creativity always appears a bit messy. It doesn't move in a linear fashion from Point A to Point B. More likely, ideas ping pong back and forth and move in a spiral process as was described earlier by Steiner (1988). Just when members feel that they are going nowhere, a great idea or solution appears from what might be viewed from the outside as chaos.

Related research (Kolb, 1992) found that autonomy, freedom to choose how they would accomplish their work, was highly important to members working on creative teams. This was expected. What was unexpected, however, was that structure from the leader also was desired (Kolb, 1993). This latter finding was at first a bit puzzling to me. As I read through the data, however, I realized that what members wanted was a framework within which they could do creative work. This has relevance for facilitators. Facilitators can provide a framework that provides some structure and frees members to focus their creative energies on the task. Using strategies that stimulate creativity and techniques that generate ideas are ways to provide a framework. The work environment also plays a role.

Importance of Work Environment

When people who work with creative people, creative and innovative teams, and creative organizations talk about work environment, they almost always talk about the development of ideas from what appears to be chaos, chance, and uncertainty. The story about the development of Post-it® Note pads by a 3M engineer who sang in a choir is legendary. "The slips of paper he used to mark the hymnals kept falling out, and it dawned on him that adhesive-backed pieces of paper might solve his problem" (Peters, 1988, p. 433). The story does not stop there. Although market surveys of the idea were negative, secretaries at 3M loved the product. Post-its® finally took off when samples were mailed to the personal secretaries of Fortune 500 CEOs using the letterhead of the 3M chairman's secretary.

Not every idea turns into a Post-it®, of course, but many ideas go through a fairly up, down, and every which way process before success. So much so that creative teams have become renowned for having their own culture—one that is far looser than what exists in the rest of the organization. In a recent review of the literature on innovation, Folkestad and Gonzalez (2010) found that environment, and especially team workspace, had a significant impact on innovation. Much of the creative work in organizations today is done on teams, but there is a need for balance between work by individuals and work by groups during the creative process. Innovation combines technical and social processes (Haragon, 2003). In brainstorming, groups of people meet to generate ideas.

Importance of brainstorming. Brainstorming was reported by Folkestad and Gonzalez (2010) as an important process for allowing team members to try out new ideas and alternatives:

> It [Brainstorming] was described as the idea engine for innovative cultures, so important that entire spaces should be dedicated to the activity, and something that innovative firms and teams need to be doing regularly. (p. 128)

In earlier work, Lafley and Charan (2008) described brainstorming as part of creating a climate that helps surface "eureka moments." This focus on the positive aspects of brainstorming is important. Brainstorming has been around for so long and is such a simple process that it may be discounted as a viable technique. Brainstorming, as well as other techniques for idea generation, are described in Chapter 12. Sufficient workspace is needed if the creative process is to be allowed to develop in its typical rather messy way; this space should allow for both individual reflection and group interaction.

Physical space requirements. Folkestad and Gonzalez (2010) identify three factors related to physical space that are important for increasing innovation among teams:

1. The nature of the space itself should be open, "providing lots of shared spaces for team meetings, spaces that approximate neighborhoods that invite collaboration, spacing for conducting brainstorming activities, and spaces that were constantly being revitalized and updated based on the project of the team members involvement or direction" (p. 128).

2. The location in inviting participation from external stakeholders is important.

3. Locating team members in these spaces over longer periods of time in order to create a creative environment is also important. "Colocation is not only about space but about time to work together and focus on a problem while retaining a commitment to external discovery and engagement" (p. 128).

Application to facilitation. Clearly, space—the right type of space—is important for the creative process. An earlier discussion in Chapter 4 talked about the importance of physically inspecting the room and the space available before agreeing on a location for a planned group work session. When creative work is involved, this step is vital. A small room or one that has a fixed arrangement of tables and desks will limit options. Several of the strategies discussed here and techniques discussed in subsequent chapters require space. Facilitators should keep this in mind when planning meetings.

Trust as Related to Idea Generation

The process of social facilitation allows for individuals to be stimulated by a group and at the same time to contribute to the shaping of the group's behavior (Sisk & Williams, 1981). During the creative process, individuals do both. They influence and are influenced by others. Psychological safety (Ulloa & Adams, 2004), the belief that risk taking is safe, enters into a group member's willingness to offer ideas and opinions that might put the person at risk of appearing foolish. Trust is a big part of this willingness.

Few team members work on activities that will lead to the development of a Post-it® Note idea, but members of most groups benefit from attempts to encourage creative thinking in their decision making, problem solving, and approaches to tasks. Rollof (2009) asked people who attended meetings in their workplace to reflect on their experiences with creativity in these meetings. Nearly all the people interviewed regarded trust as a critical factor. Without trust, they believed that new ideas would not be brought forth. Trust was covered in considerable detail in Chapter 7 in the discussion on collaborative climate. I won't repeat that discussion here, but be aware that that trust influences the extent to which people are willing to engage in the creative process with other group members. Interestingly, group members may feel most free in one of two instances: (1) when members are strangers to each other and thus don't present any barriers for open discussion and (2) when members have been together for a considerable amount of time and have developed a close working relationship. If you are working with a group that falls between these two extremes, you need to think about the inhibiting factors that may be in force and take whatever steps you can to counterbalance those factors. Having people present initial ideas privately is one way to do this. The facilitator then posts all ideas, and the creative process moves on from there.

Another influence on willingness to engage is the extent to which members believe that creativity is valued both by the group and by the organization. Assuming that there is some degree of trust and a belief that creativity is valued, a variety of strategies might be used to stimulate creativity.

The creative process might involve a free association of ideas, a process of producing ideas in rapid succession with a minimum of restraints, or a reframing of a problem that focuses attention on alternative approaches. Both strategies have been adapted from other fields of study and applied to the study and practice of small groups.

Strategies to Stimulate Creativity

Free Association. This first strategy historically is associated with Freud and the process of psychoanalysis. As applied to creative problem solving, free association is a method of stimulating the imagination to accomplish some specific purpose such as producing new combinations, intangible ideas, or names. The process begins with jotting down a symbol—a word, sketch, number, or picture—related to the problem or issue of interest. Add another symbol suggested by the first one and repeat ad lib until ideas emerge (Souder & Ziegler, 1988). Since a sketch or picture can be used instead of words, this technique works well when members are not all fluent in one language.

In this method, as contrasted with others in which the facilitator records ideas, members record their own ideas and images directly on a board or flip chart. Encourage members to help each other if someone has difficulty in expressing an idea. This process works best when used in groups of 10 or fewer. With larger groups, break into small groups and have each group go through the process. Post all ideas and then have a whole group discussion from that point. You may want to choose one of the techniques discussed in Part Three to continue developing ideas created from free association.

Creative reframing. The second strategy, creative reframing, is a process that involves a reexamination of a problem or an issue related to a problem. This process has been widely used for a number of years in psychology, sociology, counseling, conflict resolution, and negotiation. Changing the wording or the manner in which an event is described is useful when a group appears stuck or is viewing a problem in negative terms or in a way that limits progress (Simons, 1976; Kolb & Gray, 2007).

A facilitator takes control of the process by writing a problem on the left side of a board or flip chart and leaving room on the right side for reframing of the problem. Exhibit 10-1 provides examples.

Exhibit 10-1. Examples of Creative Reframing

Presenting Problem	Creative Reframing
We don't have enough resources.	How can we make better use of the resources we have?
Our goal is unachievable.	How can we break down our goal into realistic steps?
It's them.	How are we contributing to this problem?

Creative reframing can then continue by choosing a reframed statement and working on solutions for the restated or reframed problem. A criticism is that restating the problem does little to solve it. While that certainly is true, reframing the problem is a useful first step for moving groups away from roadblocks that might be limiting their thinking. The way we talk about a problem has a great deal to do with how we approach it. This process moves groups away from a focus on what can't happen to a consideration of what might be possible.

Summary

In this chapter, I defined and described creativity, discussed ways in which creativity can be developed, and explained the strategies of free association and creative reframing that can be used to stimulate creative thinking in groups. In the next chapter, I move to the process of decision making/problem solving. Subsequent chapters in Part Three describe techniques that are useful for generating and ranking ideas, focusing on problems and solutions, and strategic planning.

References

Davis, G. A. (1983). *Creativity is forever.* Dubuque, IA: Kendall/ Hunt.

DeBono, E. (1968). *New think.* New York: Basic Books.

Folkestad, J., & Gonzalez, R. (2010). Teamwork for innovation: A content analysis of the highly read and highly cited literature on innovation. *Advances in Developing Human Resources, 12*(1), 115–136.

Haragon, A. (2003). *How breakthroughs happen.* Boston: Harvard Business School Press.

Kolb, J. A. (1992). Leadership of creative teams. *Journal of Creative Behavior, 26,* 1–9.

Kolb, J. A. (1993). Leading engineering teams: Leader behaviors related to team performance. *IEEE Transactions on Professional Communication, 36,* 206–211.

Kolb, J. A. (1996). A comparison of leadership behaviors and competencies in high- and average-performance teams. *Communication Reports, 9,* 173–183.

Kolb, J. A., & Gray, B. L. (2007). Using collaborative alliances to build leadership capacity: A five-year initiative. *Central Business Review, 26*(1), 11–16.

Lafley, A., & Charan, R. (2008). *The game-changer: How you can drive revenue and profit growth with innovation.* New York: Crown Business.

Lumsden, G., & Lumsden, D. (1993). *Communicating in groups and teams: Sharing leadership.* Belmont, CA: Wadsworth.

Peters, T. J. (1988). A skunkworks tale. In R. Katz (Ed.), *Managing professionals in innovative organizations* (pp. 433–441). Cambridge, MA: Ballinger.

Rollof, J. (2009). Creative meetings. *Innovation: Management, Policy & Practice, 11*(3), 357–373.

Shapero, A. (1988). Managing creative professionals. In R. Katz (Ed.), *Managing professionals in innovative organizations* (pp. 215–222). Cambridge, MA: Ballinger.

Simon, H. A. (1987). Making management decisions: The role of intuition and emotion. *Academy of Management Executive, 1*(1), 57–64.

Simons, H. W. (1976) *Persuasion in society.* Thousand Oaks: CA: Sage.

Sisk, H, L., & Williams, J. C. (1981). *Management & organization* (4th ed). Cincinnati, OH: South-Western.

Souder, W. E., & Ziegler, R. W. (1988). A review of creativity and problem solving techniques. In R. Katz (Ed.), *Managing professionals in innovative organizations* (pp. 267–279). Cambridge, MA: Ballinger.

Steiner, G. (1988). The creative individual. In R. Katz (Ed.), *Managing professionals in innovative organizations* (pp. 201–214). Cambridge, MA: Ballinger.

Ulloa, B.C.R., & Adams, S. G. (2004). Attitude toward teamwork and effective teaming. *Team Performance Management, 10*(7/8), 145–151.

von Oech, R. (1983). *A whack on the side of the head: How to unlock your mind for innovation.* New York: Warner Books.

 **Techniques**

Key Concepts

- Definitions
- Principles for decision making/problem solving
- Why use specific techniques?
- Techniques classification and format

The previous chapter on creativity offered some ideas for stimulating and encouraging creativity. In this chapter, I first provide definitions for decision making and problem solving and then describe and discuss six general principles that can be used in determining how to best help your group with this process. Next, I talk about the use of specific techniques and explain how the techniques covered in subsequent chapters are categorized. As you read this chapter and the chapters in Part Three, realize that each technique can be modified. You may want to choose a piece of this one and add a portion of another to come up with a hybrid technique that is appropriate for your group's members and situation. First, some definitions.

Definitions

Strictly speaking, decision making is the process of choosing among alternatives. Problem solving is a multistage process for moving from an undesirable or unsatisfactory condition, situation, or state to a more desirable or satisfactory state. Put another way, the purpose in problem solving is to close the gap between what is happening now (current situation) and what we want to have happen (desired situation). Decision making is also imbedded in the problem-solving process, and I see the two as intertwined.

Principles for Decision Making and Problem Solving

As we address decision making and problem solving, there are a number of principles that will be repeated in a variety of forms and with differing levels of focus in the techniques covered in subsequent chapters. These principles are found in Exhibit 11-1.

Exhibit 11-1. Seven Principles for Structuring Problem-Solving Discussion

1. Focus on the problem before thinking and talking about how to solve it.

2. Begin with a single, unambiguous problem question.

3. Map the problem thoroughly.

4. Be sure the group members agree on criteria or ways of measuring the adequacy of decisions/ solutions.

5. Resist evaluation/judgment when gathering ideas/solutions.

6. Avoid groupthink (conformity to the beliefs of the group or its leaders) through constructive disagreement.

7. Verbally plan for implementation and follow-up of solutions.

Source: Brilhart, J. K. (1986). *Effective group discussion* (5th ed.). Dubuque, IA: Brown.

The next section clarifies what is meant by each principle and gives examples and support for the process.

Principle 1: Focus on the problem. Hirokawa (1983) provides some support for facilitators in our quest to keep groups from rushing to solutions. He found that successful problem-solving groups, as compared to unsuccessful groups, focused early in the discussion on an analysis of the problem whereas unsuccessful groups began almost immediately to evaluate solutions. Unsuccessful groups also expressed more negative emotions, possibly due to the frustration of solving a problem they did not fully understand.

Principle 2: Begin with a problem question. A problem question focuses on what's wrong. A solution question focuses on what to do. An example given by Brilhart (1986, p. 296) is as follows (italics added):

> What can be done to reduce complaints about parking space at our college? (a *problem* question, focusing on the difference between the present state of complaints and a desired state of few or no complaints)

> versus

> What can be done to get more parking space at our college? (a *solution* question, asserting indirectly that what ought to be done is create more parking spaces.
>   Maybe more beneficial in the long run would be improved public transit, off-campus classes, or shuttle busing from existing parking space elsewhere).

This principle highlights a mistake that even the most experienced facilitators can make: framing the question in a way that limits the available solutions. A great deal of time can be wasted by groups who are energetically engaged in solving the wrong problem. There's a saying in the Human Resource Development field, "If it's not a training problem, training won't fix it." After much frustration, HRD professionals have finally begun to convince managers of the need to conduct a needs analysis before assuming a problem is training related. In like manner, facilitators need to be sure that group members have a thorough understanding of the problem before they try to solve it.

Principle 3: Map the problem thoroughly. Important here is the willingness to explore any and all ideas and to gather information that is needed. No member should come forward with any preferred solution at this point. You may want to think of this step as brainstorming the problem. All relevant information should be available.

Principle 4: Be sure members agree on criteria. Setting criteria is an important step in any decision-making problem-solving situation. Group members need to agree on benchmarks or areas of importance against which solutions can be evaluated. Brilhart suggests that criteria be worded either as absolute statements, such as "must not cost over $5,000," or as questions, such as "how convenient is the location?" Some techniques such as Kepner-Tregoe have precise procedures for setting and ranking criteria and assigning numerical scores to each criteria and option. Each solution or option ultimately is evaluated in terms of how well it meets the criteria. Time should be spent on criteria since they are the backbone of a decision.

Principle 5: Defer judgment when seeking solutions. This principle is linked to Principle 3—the importance of getting all ideas on the table before beginning to evaluate them. As previously discussed, criticism of ideas is not appropriate during idea- or solution-generation steps. If there are several limits on a group's decision, however, as is often the case, you may want to consider those limitations in discussions of solutions. You would then have a free-wheeling discussion of all options that fall within certain parameters. All ideas should be encouraged and captured for future discussion.

Principle 6: Use constructive argument to avoid group think. Constructive argument, disagreement, and conflict that focuses on issues all have a positive influence on decision making and problem solving and help groups uncover, discuss, and consider all facets and ramifications. Easily reached consensus is not always a good thing. Quick agreements may mean that members have not thoroughly explored the issues involved. Having a norm of devil's advocate with members encouraged to raise negative aspects before decisions are reached is one way of helping groups avoid groupthink.

Principle 7: Verbally plan for implementation of solutions. Depending on the group's purpose, your group may or may not be charged with carrying out the solution. However, a consideration of implementation, however rudimentary, may surface problems or issues that might arise. This final step will provide some direction to subsequent groups on how to put the decisions made into effect.

Problem solving, which includes decision making, may appear quite complicated, but the process involves a series of common-sense steps. Some decisions are easy and can be made, and made well, in a few minutes. Others are more complex, more important to the group, and have lasting implications. For these complicated problems and decisions, knowledge of a variety of techniques can improve a facilitator's ability to help a group make an appropriate decision.

Why Use Specific Techniques?

Now that we've covered general principles, why can't facilitators just use these principles to help groups make decisions and solve problems. The answer is, they can. Techniques, however, provide clarity and a sense of direction for the group and make the process flow more smoothly. Techniques are useful for several reasons.

Techniques minimize process loss. During the decision-making or problem-solving process, groups follow steps, either formally or informally, that move the group toward a result. These steps increase participation among members, reduce the chance of one or two people dominating the discussion, and cover in sequence issues relevant to a full exploration of the problem. Certain factors such as varying status levels among group members, confidentiality of matters discussed, language issues, lack of experience with group decision making, and potential for high levels of disagreement may lead to process loss or a reduction in decision quality due to the process used to discuss an issue. The use of a specific technique, chosen for its relevance to the task at hand and the needs of the group, is a way to minimize process loss.

Techniques focus the group. Additionally, use of a specific technique tends to focus the group. In zero-history groups, groups meeting for the first time, the use of a specific technique will expedite goal accomplishment. The process saves time by leading members from one step to another and avoiding misdirection and the process loss mentioned above. In more established groups, a technique might serve to highlight the importance of a decision being made and cause group members to think about issues in a different way. Although techniques do not take the place of a facilitator, a technique may make it easier for the facilitator to help the group reach its goal.

Techniques have research support. People interested in decision making have been studying the results of group use of specific techniques since the late 1950s. In one early study (Maier & Maier, 1957, as cited in Brilhart, 1986), experts evaluating solutions produced by managers working collectively reported higher decision quality from the groups that used a more structured approach as compared to those that used open discussion. They also had an unexpected finding: group leaders following a more structured approach needed more tact since group members resented having to focus on one issue at a time. Things have not changed all that much in over 50 years. Facilitators doing what they feel is best for the group may encounter resistance if what they suggest goes against the group's preferred way of working. That preferred way may include lack of attention to significant issues and a premature rush to solutions. Research conducted in subsequent years (Brilhart, 1986; Janis & Mann, 1977; Schultz, Ketrow, & Urban, 1995) reported that efforts to improve decision making by the use of some structured process were successful. We cannot assume that groups intuitively know how to solve problems and make decisions. LaFasto and Larson (2001) state, "...in the area of group problem solving, a number of different problem-solving strategies have been examined over the years, and they all work better than trial and error" (p. 82).

Recent research continues to examine the balancing act between group effectiveness and member satisfaction. In one study (Salisbury, Parent, & Chin, 2008), two groups used Group System Support systems for decision making. Both groups sat at personal computers and had been previously trained in the use of GSS. In one group, members were forced by the program to complete one task before starting another. The facilitator in this first more restrictive group also made comments whenever members deviated from the steps in the process or tried to jump ahead. In a second, less restricted group, the GSS system did not control the way in which members completed their tasks. Also, the facilitator in the latter group did not comment but was only available when requested. Groups that followed the more restrictive procedure reported greater satisfaction with the process itself but less interaction among members. The researchers concluded that there are tradeoffs that should be considered when using GSS systems. Note that the restrictiveness was deliberately set quite high for first group in the Salisbury et al. study.

There are lessons that can be learned here for facilitators, regardless of technology use or type of technique. A facilitator with sufficient knowledge about group process should be able to keep a group on track when using a technique without sacrificing interaction among members—in fact some techniques require a great deal of interaction—but adherence to a technique should never become the primary concern. Techniques are tools, much as technology is a tool, and should be used as such, as a mechanism for accomplishing a group's purpose. All techniques have advantages and disadvantages, and all can be used as facilitators see fit to serve a function in a specific group situation.

Techniques serve a two-for-one purpose. Using a specific technique to help a group work through a problem accomplishes two purposes: (1) the group reaches a decision by following a series of steps that have been shown to be effective and (2) the group learns a technique that can be used again for similar situations. Facilitators are not always available to groups, and groups left to their own devices are more likely to follow effective process if they have learned a step-by-step technique. In developmental facilitation, as discussed in Chapter 1, one of the jobs of the facilitator is to teach members processes and techniques that can be used in a variety of situations.

Although most of the techniques presented in Part Three can be used in a variety of ways, I have divided them into categories that indicate areas of primary use.

How Techniques are Categorized

Techniques for idea generation. The first technique covered under idea generation, brainstorming, was mentioned in the chapter of creativity but is discussed in more depth under idea generation (Chapter 12). Brainstorming, or a variation, is used alone or as a step many different techniques. Along with Brainstorming and several modifications of this technique (reverse brainstorming, metaphors, fantasy chaining, synectics), KJ Method/Affinity and Delphi techniques are covered here.

Techniques for ranking ideas. The first technique covered, nominal group technique, was originally designed in response to criticism that brainstorming was too interactive and that periods of individual reflection would enhance the creative process. In this technique, as well as in the second technique, Kepner-Tregoe, ideas are ranked for the purposes of decision making. Kepner-Tregoe uses a precise mathematical process to calculate weights and scores for criteria and the options that are being considered. Both are discussed in Chapter 12.

Techniques that focus on the problem. Groups may begin to work on a problem before fully understanding the nature of the problem. Three techniques that focus most directly on the problem are fishbone, single question, and force-field analysis (Chapter 13).

Techniques that focus on solutions. Two techniques are highlighted here: standard agenda and program evaluation and review (Chapter 13), although most of the techniques covered in other sections also include solutions steps.

Techniques for strategic planning. Facilitators quite often are involved with strategic planning sessions. Techniques included here include SWOT (strengths, weaknesses, opportunities, and threats), appreciative inquiry, and scenario planning (Chapter 14).

Format

Each technique covered in Chapters 12, 13, and 14 is described using the following format: name and description, reference, use, materials needed, advantages, disadvantages, suggestions/ comments, and steps and/or an example. In this way, each technique is self-contained for easy use.

Summary

This chapter, techniques, is the last element in the Framework for Facilitation presented in Chapter 3. In Part Three, we turn to coverage of the techniques mentioned here. After setting the stage for decision making and problem solving in this chapter, Chapter 12 focuses on idea generation, which may be used alone or as a first step in a process, and then to ranking of ideas and suggestions.

References

Brilhart, J. K. (1986). *Effective group discussion* (5th ed.). Dubuque, IA: Brown.

Hirokawa, R. Y. (1983). Group communication and problem solving effectiveness: An investigation of group phases, *Human Communication Research, 9,* 291–305.

Janis, I. L., & Mann, L. (1977). *Decision-making: a psychological analysis of conflict, choice, and commitment.* New York: Free Press.

LaFasto, M. J., & Larson, C. E. (2001). *When teams work best.* Thousand Oaks, CA: Sage.

Maier, N.R.F., & Maier, R. A. (1957). An experimental test of the effects of "development" vs. "free" discussions on the quality of group decisions. *Journal of Applied Psychology, 41,* 320–323.

Salisbury, W. D., Parent, M., & Chin, W. W. (2008). Robbing Peter to pay Paul: The differential effect of GSS restrictiveness on process satisfaction and group cohesion. *Group Decision and Negotiation, 17,* 303–320.

Schultz, B., Ketrow, S. M., & Urban, D. M. (1995). Improving decision quality in the small group: The role of the reminder. *Small Group Research, 26,* 521–541.

Part Three
Techniques

12

Techniques for Generating and Ranking Ideas

Key Concepts

- Techniques for generating ideas
  - Brainstorming and variations
  - KJ Method/Affinity
  - Delphi
- Techniques for ranking ideas and options
  - Nominal Group
  - Modified Kepner-Tregoe

In the last chapter, I talked about general principles for decision making and problem solving and explained why the use of specific techniques are useful in helping groups move through this process. In this chapter, I describe techniques to be used for idea generation and idea ranking. As a reminder, each of these techniques can be pulled apart and combined to create a process that works best for your group. I start with techniques for idea generation.

Techniques for Generating Ideas

When we think of creativity and specifically of generating ideas, the brainstorming process most often comes to mind. Brainstorming has been in use for a long time, and many processes today use some version of brainstorming as a first step in creative thinking. Several variations of brainstorming have been proposed and are discussed in the following section.

Brainstorming

Name and Description

Brainstorming was developed by advertising executive, Alex Osborn, as a technique for encouraging creative thought around a stated goal or purpose. The focus is on quantity versus quality of ideas. A primary principle is that criticism and evaluation of ideas should be avoided.

References

Jewell, L., & Reitz, J. (1988). Group decision making. In R. Katz (Ed.), *Managing professionals in innovative organizations* (pp. 247–261). Cambridge, MA: Ballinger.

Osborn, A. F. (1957). *Applied imagination: Principles and procedures of creative problem solving* (rev. ed). New York: Scribner.

Use

To generate as many ideas as possible within a stated time frame; to jump start a discussion; often appears as one step or component in other decision-making or problem-solving techniques

Materials Needed

- A large space to visually display the ideas: blackboard, whiteboard, or flip chart paper that can be posted as sheets are filled
- Markers, chalk

Advantages

Can create enthusiasm in group members about number of possible options. The visual display might encourage members to offer novel ideas.

Disadvantages

Ideas generated may be irrelevant. Some people may become competitive in offering ideas; others may not speak at all.

Brainstorming, alone, does not lead to closure. Additional discussion is needed to evaluate and choose solutions.

Suggestions/Comments

To increase members' creativity, give them advance notice and suggest they think about the issue before the session. Facilitators need to capture the essence of an idea and record it quickly. During the session, it is helpful to have two people recording ideas and two flip charts; while one person is finishing writing one idea, the other can be capturing the next. The facilitator may be one of the recorders or may direct the process.

Round robin expression of ideas (one person at a time moving in a set sequence around the room) encourages full participation, but might inhibit the free-flowing nature of the process.

Rules for Traditional Brainstorming

Rules for brainstorming have appeared in various forms since this technique was developed; the following four rules capture the essence of the process.

1. Avoid criticism of ideas. Facilitators should remind any member who violates this rule.

2. Quantity of ideas is desired. The more suggestions, the better.

3. Encourage extreme or outlandish ideas. No idea is too ridiculous.

4. Building upon one anothers' ideas is welcome. This is called hitchhiking or piggybacking. Combining ideas is important because it encourages active listening and results in synthesis and expansion of ideas.

Variations of Brainstorming

Reverse Brainstorming

A form of brainstorming also called a tear-down or purge method consists of being critical instead of suspending judgment and may be used prior to a typical brainstorming session. "A typical approach would be to first list all the things wrong with the operation, process, system, or product. Then, one would systematically take each flaw uncovered and suggest ways of overcoming, improving, or correcting it" (Souder & Ziegler, 1988, p. 268). If not managed correctly, this type of session can become overly negative with flaws becoming too important.

Use of Metaphors

A variation of brainstorming that phrases comparisons between two things as if one thing were the other. Lumsden and Lumsden (1993) describe one example of using metaphorical thinking to help a team that is having trouble working together. Members might describe themselves as "discordant" or "off key" (p. 158). Someone might pick up on the musical metaphor and talk about members playing on a different place on the score or the team not having a conductor. Metaphors can trigger insights and possibilities.

Fantasy Chaining

A form of brainstorming that uses a "spontaneously emerging story or drama to help a group unfold or describe a situation or problem. Group members build on the ideas of others to develop a chain of events" (Shockley-Zalabak, 1995, p. 331). As a group develops a situation in a format resembling a play, ideas and insights may emerge.

Synectics

A facilitated brainstorm process approach that uses both metaphors and fantasy chaining. Group members explore problems in terms of what the problem is also like and how it can best be described. Shockley-Zalabak (p. 331) gives an example of helping a group understand an air traffic control system by describing how schools of fish swim without bumping into one another. This process can help a group develop alternative approaches.

The next technique is also a version of brainstorming, but this time, the process is extended by sorting the ideas produced by brainstorming into categories.

KJ Method/Affinity Technique

Name and Description

KJ Method, also called affinity technique and affinity diagram, was created by Japanese anthropologist Jiro Kawakita. This process relies upon intuitive, nonlogical thinking processes and encourages group involvement. Group members work individually to generate ideas and then at a board or other large surface with other group members to sort these ideas into groups or categories that have points of similarity or affinity that tie the ideas together.

References

Kawakita, J. (1982). *The original KJ-method.* Tokyo, Japan: Kawakita Research Institute.

Scupin, R. (1997). The KJ method: A technique for analyzing data derived from Japanese ethnology. *Human Organization 56*(2), 233–237.

Use

Although originally designed as a method for sorting research data, can be used also to sort ideas generated through brainstorming or similar activities into a series of themes or categories. Useful when there are a large number of ideas.

Materials Needed

- Large work surface that can be used to post notes
- Stick-on notes or large cards; markers
- At times the notes remain posted for a while, allowing members to move individual cards over a period of time until all are satisfied; a large board in a common work area is ideal for this purpose

Advantages

Builds teamwork. Group members may come to a better understanding of the ideas through the sorting process. Physical movement involved in moving to the board provides a break from sitting that may also encourage creativity. The facilitator does not need to record ideas.

Disadvantages

Can be time consuming when large amounts of data are involved. Some people may have difficulty expressing their ideas briefly in writing.

Suggestions/Comments

Allow plenty of time for the categorization process. If board is placed in a group meeting place, members can work on this over several days. Others can see the work in process, which may generate new ideas. When used in a group session with more than 10 people, work in small groups first and then combine the efforts.

Steps

1. The same rules are used as those listed previously for traditional brainstorming. Instead of orally stating ideas that are recorded by a facilitator, members write each idea on a separate card or slip of paper that can be attached to a board. The facilitator may specify a maximum number of ideas per person or leave the number open.

2. Members come to the board and post their cards or slips in random order on the board.

3. Members work individually and then collectively to decide on placement of ideas into certain categories or themes that appear to capture the essence of the ideas placed in the category.

The last technique in this section is used to bring together for a specific purpose individuals who, either by choice or circumstance, work at a distance from each other. The easy availability of electronic communication today has caused a resurgence of this method that initially used surface mail to distribute packets of information to participants.

Delphi Technique

Name and Description

Delphi technique was developed by researchers at Rand Corporation for the purpose of providing members with ideas and evaluative feedback from each other while avoiding the inefficiency and inhibitions of face-to-face groups. Delphi is used today to obtain information from a number of experts who may be scattered all over the world. The group members never meet face-to-face. Rather, all their interaction is through their responses to a Delphi questionnaire.

References

Dalkey, N. C., Rourke, D. L., Lewis, R., & Snyder, D. (1972). *Studies in the quality of life: Delphi and decision making.* Lexington, MA: Heath.

Delbecq, A. L., Van de Ven, A. H., & Gustafson, D. H. (1975). *Group techniques for program planning: A guide to nominal group and delphi processes.* Glenview, IL: Scott Foresman.

Use

For situations in which face-to-face interaction is not desired because of past or potential problems with members communicating effectively or not possible without great expense such as when group members are at a distance. Allows for inclusion of a variety of experts or points of view. Members may be anonymous. Questionnaire is distributed until consensus is reached.

Materials Needed

Depends on technology used; at minimum, you need e-mail addresses for each participant to allow for distribution and return of materials. Responses could be posted on web site anonymously by members and then summarized and posted for member access by facilitator. Questionnaire itself could be posted and completed electronically.

Advantages

Removes usual group restraints on communication and allows for the full experience, expertise, and critical ability of participants to be brought to bear. Eliminates the cost of bringing the group together. Prevents domination by one person. Reduces the likelihood of groupthink since members do not develop relationships with each other beyond what is needed for the process.

Disadvantages

Can be time consuming if questionnaire responses are summarized and returned to members multiple times. People may drop out. Depends in large part of the skill of the person(s) summarizing the responses. Respondents with poor writing skills or those who are communicating in other than their primary language may create responses that are difficult to interpret.

Suggestions/Comments

A modification has less emphasis on summaries compiled by a facilitator. Responses are shared with the group as is. Adequate writing skills in one common language are even more necessary, however, with less involvement from a facilitator. Regardless of how summaries are compiled, keeping participants engaged throughout the process is important to minimize dropouts. If consensus is not necessary, the procedure could be shortened.

There are variations in the Delphi process depending on the extent of the involvement of a facilitator, group, or other people in preparing and summarizing results of the rounds. The following basic steps are generally included:

Steps

1. Facilitator or small group designs a questionnaire that is to be completed by a larger Delphi group.

2. Questionnaire is distributed.

3. Round 1 of questionnaire is completed and returned.

4. Results are compiled and distributed to all members of the Delphi group. Ideas or solutions are listed without any identifying information.

5. Second questionnaire is completed and returned.

6. Process continues until consensus.

Techniques for Ranking Ideas and Options

Although the two techniques covered in this section are complete processes, they each focus on ranking options and ultimately making a decision based on that ranking. The first is nominal group technique.

Nominal Group Technique

Name and Description

Nominal group technique, developed by Delbecq and Van de Ven, combines periods of individuals working individually with periods of group discussion. The name reflects the limited or nominal interaction required. The technique consists of six steps and involves a process of private voting and ranking of ideas and solutions. The technique may be easily modified in ways that increase the confidentiality of responses.

Reference

Delbecq, A. L., Van de Ven, A. H., & Gustafson, D. H. (1975). *Group techniques for program planning: A guide to nominal group and delphi processes.* Glenview, IL: Scott Foresman.

Uses

For situations in which participation from all is desired but factors within the situation or member population may inhibit responses. The silent reflection portion of this technique fosters creativity. The privacy of some of the steps is particularly good for situations and/or groups in which tension levels are high or groups in which status differences, cultural diversity, or use of English as a second language might result in unequal participation.

Materials Needed

- Flip chart, blackboard, whiteboard, or computer screen that can be used to record responses
- Markers
- Index cards for writing ideas and voting
- Handouts to record comments and ideas
- Stick-on dots for voting

Advantages

Reflection and round robin steps encourage creativity and involvement of those members who are often left out when a process starts with an immediate request for ideas. Reflection allows individuals time to gather their thoughts.

Voting protects privacy so that responses are more likely to be honest in sensitive situations. Members are less subject to influence by others than in some other techniques.

Disadvantages

Limits full discussion. Some topics would benefit from an open discussion of issues and opinions. Less group energy than in more interactive techniques. Voting can be time consuming. See suggestions.

Suggestions/Comments

A modification to Step 2 would increase confidentiality of responses. Members submit ideas on cards to the facilitator or an assistant who then writes them on a board. Alternatively, ideas can be submitted electronically or in some other way to facilitator in advance of the meeting. The meeting would then begin with all the ideas generated by members posted and available on handouts.

Time taken with voting can be reduced by having participants vote using stick-on dots. Each member is given three (or whatever number seems appropriate) dots and asked to vote by placing one dot by three of the posted choices.

Generally the rule is that all three dots cannot be placed on one idea or solution. Decide ahead of time what makes sense and rely on people's integrity since you do not want to have people vote one at a time. Choices made by members are seen by others, so privacy is lost. This may or may not matter depending on sensitivity of issue.

The nominal group technique continues until a decision is reached. The following steps are involved:

Steps

1. Silent individual generation of ideas in writing.

2. Round-robin reporting of ideas that are then recorded by the facilitator on a flip chart or board so that everyone can see them. There is no discussion during the recording of ideas.

3. Clarification of ideas or solution—facilitator takes the group through the list item by item. Anyone may ask another person for clarification of an idea. Evaluative comments are discouraged.

4. Silent ranking of ideas—each person is given a set of note cards or slips of paper on which to write the items he or she most prefers. Depending on the situation, the five (or what-ever number appears logical) most preferred ideas are recorded, one per paper or card, and ranked (with five cards, five would be the highest rating and one the lowest) by each individual. Cards are collected and scores for each idea calculated. These rankings are recorded where the entire group can see them. (The technique may stop here if the group has agreed on a course of action. If not, the pro-cedure continues.)

5. Discussion of priorities—discussion ensues for the several items having the highest scores. This should be an evaluative discussion with critical examination of ideas encouraged.

6. Repeat step 4—rerank ideas. Continue Steps 5 and 6 until either a few ideas have surfaced or one solution has emerged.

This next method also includes voting but uses a mathematical model and, additionally, stresses the use of criteria as discussed in the prior chapter.

Modified Kepner-Tregoe Method

Name and Description

Modified Kepner-Tregoe Method. This technique, modified from the decision analysis process developed by Kepner-Tregoe in 1981, uses a mathematical process to come to a group decision. Particular emphasis is placed on setting criteria and then evaluating each option against that criteria. My slight modification of Kepner-Tregoe, as well as their full process, are both explained under Steps.

Reference

Kepner, C. H., & Tregoe, B. B. (1981). *The new rational manager.* Princeton, N.J.: Princeton Research Press.

Use

When a choice among alternatives needs to be made and when the situation lends itself to ranking of criteria and options. Works best when each option involves several pieces of detailed information that can be used for ranking purposes.

Materials Needed

- Flip chart, blackboard, whiteboard, or computer screen that can be used to record responses
- Markers
- Handouts
- Calculator

Advantages

Puts importance on criteria setting, an important aspect of decision making. Forces members to distinguish between necessary and desired criteria (needs and wants). Follows a clear procedure that can be documented and explained.

Disadvantages

Ranking one option against another is difficult in some types of situations. Some members dislike the mathematical nature of this technique because they either don't like dealing with numbers or they believe assigning numbers is either distasteful or inappropriate.

Suggestions/Comments

Decisions depend on careful attention to criteria setting and numbers assigned to importance of criteria. If members don't like the final decision, there is a good chance that they did not devote sufficient time to setting criteria. If a criterion is listed as necessary, any option not fitting that criterion is eliminated from consideration. Facilitators must make sure that members understand this. The facilitator will need help when moving through this technique. Either work with a cofacilitator or an assistant or ask group members to become involved in adding scores.

This technique or a variation is very useful when groups need to compare alternatives. If you use it to rank people across criteria, information that can be quantified such as years of experience or level of education is less subject to criticism.

Steps

1. Begin with a clear decision statement.

2. Establish criteria for the decision (both *needs* and *wants*); what is essential; what is desirable.

3. Establish weights for each criterion (a scale of 1–10 with 10 being highest allows for substantial variation in importance of each criterion). For example, a group may be choosing a site for a new office building. If location adjacent to a highway is an important criterion, location may be given a weight of 9.

4. Evaluate alternatives against established criteria. If a location adjacent to a highway is considered a *need,* any alternative that does not meet this criterion is eliminated from consideration. The remaining alternatives are scored for this and other criteria and ranked against each other. For example, if you have five alternatives, the one with the best location is given a 10, the second an 8, others a 6, 4, and 2 (depending on the degree of difference between the alternatives). The location scores for the five alternatives in the example would be 90, 72, 54, 36, and 18, respectively.

5. Complete the rankings on all criteria and choose the "best" alternative (the one with the highest overall score).

6. Reflect on the outcome and process and determine whether additional discussion is warranted.

*__Note:__ As originally described by Kepner-Tregoe, the focus is not only on the best decision or solution to a problem but also the safest. After following a *needs* and *wants* process as described in the steps above, every alternative is then assessed as to possible adverse consequences and assigned either numerical ranking scores following the process used with *wants,* or labeled either high, medium, or low in each of two categories: probability for negative consequences and seriousness of these consequences. Depending on the purpose for which you choose to use Kepner-Tregoe, you might want to add this negative consequences step. I've found that groups often include an aspect of negative consequences in their criteria. An example of this would be *dependability* in a decision regarding technology. For some systems, a 24/7 on-call service would be listed as a *Need* because of the negative consequences associated with system failure. When used as a problem analysis technique, an assessment of the negative consequences and seriousness of possible solutions might keep a group from moving too quickly to choose a solution.

Summary

Five techniques—brainstorming, KJ Method/affinity, Delphi, nominal group technique, and Modified Kepner-Tregoe—plus four variations to brainstorming were covered in this chapter. In Chapter 13, the focus is on identification of problems and assessment of solutions.

References

Dalkey, N. C., Rourke, D. L., Lewis, R., & Snyder, D. (1972). *Studies in the quality of life: Delphi and decision making.* Lexington, MA: Heath.

Delbecq, A. L., Van de Ven, A. H., & Gustafson, D. H. (1975). *Group techniques for program planning: A guide to nominal group and delphi processes.* Glenview, IL: Scott Foresman.

Jewell, L., & Reitz, J. (1988). Group decision making. In R. Katz (Ed.), *Managing professionals in innovative organizations* (pp. 247–261). Cambridge, MA: Ballinger.

Kepner, C. H., & Tregoe, B. B. (1981). *The new rational manager.* Lumsden, G., & Lumsden, D. (1993). *Communicating in groups and teams: Sharing leadership.* Belmont, CA: Wadsworth. Princeton, NJ: Princeton Research Press.

Kawakita, J. (1982). *The original KJ-method*. Tokyo, Japan: Kawakita Research Institute.

Osborn, A. F. (1957). *Applied imagination: Principles and procedures of creative problem solving* (rev. ed.). New York: Scribner.

Scupin, R. (1997). The KJ method: A technique for analyzing data derived from Japanese ethnology. *Human Organization 56*(2), 233–237.

Shockley-Zalabak, P. (1995). *Fundamentals of organizational communicating: Knowledge, sensitivity, skills, values* (3rd ed.). White Plains, NY: Longman.

Souder, W. E., & Ziegler, R. W. (1988). A review of creativity and problem solving techniques. In R. Katz (Ed.), *Managing professionals in innovative organizations* (pp. 267–279). Cambridge, MA: Ballinger.

Techniques for Focusing on Problems and Solutions

13

Key Concepts

- Techniques for focusing on the problem
  - Fishbone diagram
  - Single question
  - Force-field analysis
- Techniques for focusing on solutions
  - Standard agenda
  - Program evaluation and review

The past chapter covered techniques that are useful for idea generation and ranking. In this chapter, I describe techniques that focus on problems and solutions. Again, most of these techniques have multiple uses. I have placed them into categories that I hope will be useful to you in determining which technique is most suitable for a particular group situation.

Techniques for Focusing on the Problem

Although we assume that groups understand the problems they face or are charged with solving, that is not always the case. Keeping groups from rushing to judgment is one of the most difficult jobs of a facilitator. This first technique focuses on identifying the root causes of a problem.

Fishbone Diagram

Name and Description

Fishbone diagram, so named because it resembles the skeleton of a fish, is a highly visual technique used to identify and organize potential causes of problems. It is also called a Ishikawa diagram, cause-and-effect diagram, and root cause diagram. This technique was first employed by Kaoru Ishikawa in the 1960s.

References

Ishikawa, K. (1982). *Guide to quality control* (2nd rev. ed.) Tokyo, Japan: Asian Productivity Organization.

Ishikawa, K. (1990). *Introduction to quality control* (3rd ed.). London, UK: Chapman & Hall.

Use

To investigate and categorize root causes of a problem. Primarily used to analyze problems in safety, health, environment, quality, reliability, and production or in any situation that lends itself to a problem statement. Group members collectively must possess specific information on all aspects of the problem.

Materials Needed

- A large space that can be used to display and then add to components of the fish. Flip chart paper generally does not provide enough space, although pages can be combined. A large blackboard or whiteboard space is preferable.
- Markers or chalk
- Handouts are a good idea so that members have the fishbone format in front of them as well as a space to write ideas and notes.

Advantages

Visually displays and organizes information and shows the linkages between the problem and its possible causes. Number of twigs used is limited only by size of fish and space available. All causes can be displayed.

Disadvantages

Need sufficient space or computer display visible to all. Members may become frustrated at having to put their ideas on a specific twig. Some problems can be listed on more than one twig, which can be a bit confusing and also takes time. See suggestion that follows. This technique focuses only on the problem. Once the problem is diagrammed, another technique or process needs to be used for solutions.

Suggestions/Comments

This technique works best with 10 or fewer people. If you choose to use in larger groups, you might want to have groups brainstorm, perhaps in dyads, on items for twigs before moving to the fishbone diagram. This eliminates some of the confusion for group members and also makes the process more manageable for the facilitator.

Keep the fatigue factor in mind. This process is best used when a clear distinction can be made for branches. I suggest a trial run before using to be sure that you understand the process and that this technique will work well for the problem at hand.

Steps

1. Decide on the problem to improve or control.

2. Draw an arrow from the left to the right side. Write the problem in a box at the tip of the arrow.

3. Choose major categories (labels) of factors that may be causing the problem. Write each category at the end of a branch coming off the main arrow.*

4. Generate causal factors for each category. Write these as twigs on each major branch. Use still smaller twigs branching off from these twigs if further details are necessary.

5. The diagram is complete when all probable factors related to the problem have been included.

*In traditional use, terms started with the same letter. Examples include Surroundings, Suppliers, Systems, and Skills; Machines, Methods, Materials, and Measures; and People, Processes, Place, Procedures, and Product. Although these terms may be easy to remember, they aren't always the best choice for a particular situation.

Figure 13-1 shows a typical fishbone diagram that charts some potential causes of a problem related to equipment failure. As an example, one potential causal factor is listed for each of four branches: People, Methods, Materials, and Measures. Additional information is added until all possible factors have been included.

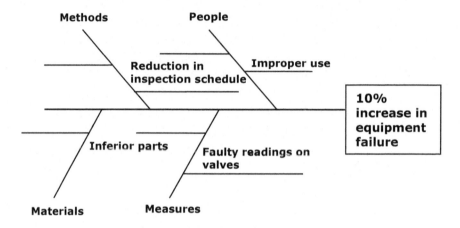

Figure 13-1. Fishbone Diagram

A second technique that focuses members' attention on the problem at hand is the single question technique. This technique, in contrast to the fishbone, includes a solutions step.

Single Question

Name and Description

Single Question. Process first developed by Carl Larson in 1969 consists of a series of central questions and sub-questions that helps groups narrow the focus of a problem. The original technique had five questions; revisions in 1983 and 2001 by Larson and Frank LaFasto changed the questions slightly, added a question on creating a collaborative climate, and included a greater emphasis on facts.

Reference

LaFasto, M. J., & Larson, C. E. (2001). *When teams work best.* Thousand Oaks, CA: Sage.

Use

To encourage a clear focus on the problem by taking a group through a series of questions that examine the problem and lead to a solution.

Materials Needed

- Flip chart, blackboard, whiteboard, or computer screen that can be used to record responses
- Markers
- Handouts

Advantages

Series of questions are designed to prevent premature problem solving. Step 2 on creating a collaborative setting is good for zero-history groups. Questions can easily be divided for use in more than one session.

Disadvantages

Collaborative climate question is time consuming and parts of it may be unnecessary for groups that have a history of working well together.

Suggestions/Comments

Decide if all questions are essential for your group. Established groups might be able to agree to (or omit) principles for discussion or the facilitator might post principles for groups and invite additions or discussion.

Steps

1. Identify the problem.
    What is the single question, the answer to which all the group needs to know to accomplish its purpose?

2. Create a collaborative setting.
    What principles should we agree on in order to maintain a reasonable and collaborative approach throughout the process? **Examples:** *invite and understand all points of view; remain fact-based in our judgments; be tough on the issues, not on each other; put aside any personal agenda.*

    What assumptions and biases are associated with the single question identified in Step 1, and how might they influence the discussion? **Examples:** *assume we know our customers' needs, believe we have efficient processes, think our level of customer service is acceptable, assume our past approach should be our future strategy.*

3. Identify and analyze the issues (subquestions).
    Before responding to the single question in Step 1, what issues, or subquestions, must be answered in order to fully understand the complexities of the overall problem?

    Additional directions: *limit opinions by focusing on the facts, if facts are unavailable, agree on the most reasonable response to each subquestion.*

    Subquestion: Relevant Facts: Best Response:

4. Identify possible solutions.
    Based on an analysis of the issues, what are the two or three most reasonable solutions to the problem?

    Possible solution: Advantages: Disadvantages:

5. Resolve the single question.
    Among the possible solutions, which one is most desirable?

The last technique in this section focuses on the desired or ideal state and the disparity that exists between that and current conditions. Although most frequently used in change efforts, it also has applications for problem solving.

Force-Field Analysis

Name and Description

Kurt Lewin developed force-field analysis in 1951 as a technique for assessing the perceived disparity between the current state and a desired or ideal state. Two sets of counterbalancing forces maintain the disparity.

This technique originated from a physics law which states that there is always as much reaction as action. Thus, all problems have positive factors as well as negative factors and these two factors work together. According to the law, driving/impelling forces and restraining/constraining forces compete. Discussions center on ways to maximize the positives and minimize the negatives.

References

Frey, L. R., & Barge, J. K. (1997). *Managing group life: Communicating in decision-making groups.* Boston: Houghton Mifflin.

Lewin, K. (1951). *Field theory in social research.* New York: Harper & Row.

Uses

To identify positive (driving) and negative (restraining) forces that affect the problem at hand. To assess factors that will help and hinder a change effort.

Materials Needed

- Flip chart, blackboard, whiteboard, or computer screen that can be used to record responses
- Markers
- Handouts

Advantages

Has visual appeal similar to fishbone diagram. Many people have heard of this technique even if they are not familiar with the details of use.

Disadvantages

Facilitator needs to be well versed in facilitating this technique in order to help members avoid pitfalls such as listing the same factors but in different words as both driving and restraining forces.

Suggestions/Comments

Advance preparation allows members to give thought to factors. Consider beginning the meeting with a few factors already posted to jump start this process.

Figure 13-2 shows the equilibrium maintained by counter-balancing driving and restraining forces in force-field analysis.

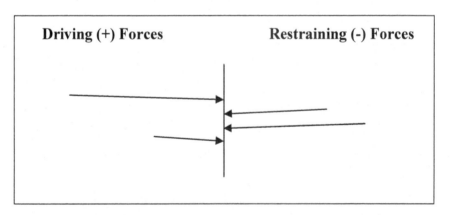

Figure 13-2. Force-Field Analysis

Definition of Terms

Driving forces—factors that are supportive in achieving desired changes.

Restraining forces—factors that can restrain or decrease the driving forces.

Equilibrium—the state reached when the sum of the driving forces equals the sum of the restraining forces. To move forward toward desired change, the relationship between driving and restraining forces must change.

Steps

1. Define problem or condition and desired state.

2. Identify driving and restraining forces.

3. Discuss the magnitude of each force or assign a number to each that indicates the perceived strength of its effect.

4. Consider the magnitude of driving and restraining forces to get an idea of the difficulty of moving toward a desired state. If you assigned a number to each force, add positive and negative numbers.

5. Once the problem is clear, discuss ways to alter forces to move toward the desired state.

6. Decide on a course of action.

   The techniques in the next section have the solution or implementation stage as a primary focus.

Techniques for Focusing on Solutions

This first technique follows a step-by-step series of questions that leads group members to a complete analysis of a situation including an assessment of the solution.

Standard Agenda

Name and Description

Standard agenda technique is based on the reflective thinking process originally identified and developed by John Dewey in 1910. It encourages external fact finding and incorporates evaluation of the solution into the process.

References

Shockley-Zalabak, P. (1995). *Fundamentals of organizational communication* (3rd ed.). White Plains, NY: Longman Publishers.

Wood, J. T., Phillips, G. M., & Pederson, D. J. (1986). *A practical guide to participation and leadership* (2nd ed.). New York: Harper & Row.

Use

When members lack comprehensive knowledge of a problem. Includes both an analysis of root causes of a problem and an assessment of solutions.

Materials Needed

- Flip chart, blackboard, whiteboard, or computer screen that can be used to lead the group through the steps
- Markers
- Handouts

Advantages

Focus on fact finding and building evaluation of the solution into the steps makes this a complete problem-to-solution model.

Disadvantages

The series of questions may seem extensive. This technique should be used when a solution is expected but details are missing in the original charge to the group.

Suggestions/Comments

The questions can be adapted to fit your group. If you have used another method (such as fishbone diagram) to define the problem, you could begin this technique at Step 4.

Identifying a series of questions that need to be answered is an important takeaway concept from this technique.

Steps

The six steps of standard agenda are in the form of a series of questions as listed below.

1. **Understanding the charge.** Why is the group in existence? What is it to do? What output is expected? What happens to the output?

2. **Understanding and phrasing the question.** What precisely is the group to examine or inquire about? Is the wording of the question clear to everyone?

3. **Fact finding.** What are the symptoms of the problem? What is the cause of the symptoms? What is happening that should not be happening?

4. **Setting criteria and limitations.** What is possible (as opposed to desirable)? What limits are there on this decision? What would a solution look like?

5. **Discovering and selecting solutions.** What are the alternatives? How does each meet the goal? What provides more of what is wanted with the least new harm? What do we know about details of the solution? What will it cost? How will we measure effectiveness of the solution?

6. **Preparing and presenting the final report.** What should be included in the report or other deliverable? How, when, and to whom should it be presented?

The next technique focuses on implementation of a decision and is generally used for long-range planning of an event or program.

Program Evaluation and Review Technique (PERT)

Name and Description

The program and review technique, known by the initials PERT, was first developed to assist the Navy Polaris missile program and has since been used by many industries in situations that involve extensive planning. It involves identifying all the events that must take place in sequence for a particular final event or accomplishment; estimating the time, materials, and people needed at each point of the process; and using this information to develop a comprehensive plan.

References

Phillips, G. M. (1973). *Communication and the small group.* Indianapolis, IN: Bobbs-Merrill.

Ross, R. S. (1989). *Small groups in organizational settings.* Englewood Cliffs, NJ: Prentice-Hall.

Use

To assess the adequacy of program or event planning prior to implementation particularly if implementation poses a significant risk or involves a considerable amount of money.

Materials Needed

- A large space is needed to diagram the process
- Blackboard, whiteboard, or computer screen can be used
- Markers
- Handouts
- Computer programs are available and suggested for extensive projects

Advantages

Focus on logistics of implementation can keep a group from making a mistake that is costly. Identification of time, materials, and people required at each step or event reduces the likelihood that details will be overlooked.

Disadvantages

More elaborate than is needed for most group projects. Should only be used for programs or events that justify the expenditure of member time.

Suggestions/Comments

This technique requires precise information. A shortened version showing the connection between events and a timeline linking events in a sequence can be used for programs not requiring this level of detail. Groups wanting to use the full process would benefit from training in its use.

Steps

The PERT process begins when the group has completed the problem-solving process and has phased the solution as a program or action to be implemented. The following nine steps capture the sequence of events.

1. Specify the final event that signals completion of the program.

2. List events that must happen before the final event and assign reference numbers.

3. Determine preceding necessary events with time attached to each.

4. Draw a PERT diagram showing connection of events. Extraneous and redundant events are deleted.

5. List activities between each pair of events.

6. Make best, worst, and most likely time estimates for activities; calculate time estimates in days for each track and variances for each event; and sum each event to determine expected completion time.

7. Determine scheduled completion date.

8. Calculate slack time for each track to final event. Draw a critical path based on path with least slack time.

9. Make estimate of satisfactory completion based on critical path.

Summary

This chapter described five techniques: three that focus on the problem—fishbone, single question, and force-field analysis—and two that focus on solutions—standard agenda and program evaluation and review (PERT). Single question and force-field analysis also include solutions or applications steps. The final technique chapter reviews three techniques suitable for strategic planning.

References

Dewey, J. (1910). *How we think*. Boston: Heath.

Frey, L. R. & Barge, J. K. (1997). *Managing group life: Communicating in decision making groups*. Boston: Houghton Mifflin.

Ishikawa, K. (1982). *Guide to quality control* (2nd rev. ed.) Tokyo, Japan: Asian Productivity Organization.

Ishikawa, K. (1990). *Introduction to quality control* (3rd ed.). London: Chapman & Hall.

LaFasto, M. J., & Larson, C. E. (2001). *When teams work best*. Thousand Oaks, CA: Sage.

Lewin, K. (1951). *Field theory in social research*. New York: Harper & Row.

Phillips, G. M. (1973). *Communication and the small group.* Indianapolis, IN: Bobbs-Merrill.

Ross, R. S. (1989). *Small groups in organizational settings.* Englewood Cliffs, NJ: Prentice-Hall.

Shockley-Zalabak, P. (1995). *Fundamentals of organizational communication* (3rd ed.). White Plains, NY: Longman.

Wood, J. T., Phillips, G. M., & Pederson, D. J. (1986). *A practical guide to participation and leadership* (2nd ed.). New York: Harper & Row.

Techniques for Strategic Planning

Key Concepts

- What is strategic planning?
- Focus on analysis
  - SWOT (strengths, weaknesses, opportunities, threats)
- Focus on possibilities
  - Appreciative inquiry
- Focus on uncertainty
  - Scenario planning
- Group goal setting

This final techniques chapter focuses on the strategic planning process. Although strategic planning sessions are prevalent, they are not always popular because of the work involved and the feelings of "Didn't we just do this?" and "What happened to our last plan?" The techniques included here might help this often-maligned process move more smoothly. First, a brief discussion of strategic planning.

What is Strategic Planning?

Strategic planning is the process of determining the major objectives of an organization and defining the strategies that will govern the acquisition and utilization of resources to accomplish those objectives.

(Schermerhorn, 1984, p. 145)

Although strategic planning can focus on a problem or a performance gap, most usually the purpose is to think ahead to factors that are likely to have an impact on the group, department, or organization over a designated period of time, generally three years. Often there are numerous strategic plans with each one coordinated with that of the larger unit. Thus a program's strategic plan is incorporated into that of a department, a department's plan is funneled into that of a larger organizational unit, and so on. If the process works appropriately, the plans are linked to each other in meaningful ways and serve to focus each unit within an organization on common goals.

The reason that facilitators are asked to help with strategic planning issues is that the process seems daunting. When faced with what seems like a monumental task and a short deadline, many groups lose focus. A facilitator can help a group formulate an approach and develop a plan that is in line with expectations. Most usually, work is done both outside and within scheduled strategic planning sessions. The success of the group depends on the willingness of the participants to create a meaningful plan, the practicality of the process outlined by the organization, and the facilitator's understanding of the organization's process and the format required for the plan.

In some cases, groups meet regularly to forecast needs and plan for the future. If this is done outside a formalized strategic planning effort, the facilitator has greater leeway in determining a plan of action that will help the group accomplish its goals for the session.

Schermerhorn (1984, p. G-15) lists four principles that apply to strategy and objectives:

1. must direct effort toward accomplishment of the organization's basic mission and overall purpose

2. should target effort on specific results that will solve key problems and exploit key opportunities in the organization's external environment

3. should build on strengths and minimize weaknesses in the organization

4. should be consistent with prevailing managerial values and the corporate culture

Three techniques are particularly useful for long-range planning purposes. Each has a specific focus.

Focus on Analysis

The first technique in this chapter is the most well known and focuses on both the external and internal environment mentioned in the principles. SWOT is a method of studying an organization's resources and capabilities to assess strengths and weaknesses and scanning its environment to identify opportunities and threats.

SWOT—Strengths, Weaknesses, Opportunities, Threats

Name and Description

SWOT was developed at Stanford Research Institute in the 1960s in research funded by Fortune 500 companies that were interested in exploring ways in which the corporate planning process could be improved. The SWOT technique that emerged from this research assesses strengths and weaknesses originating in the internal environment and identifies opportunities and threats from the external environment.

References

Capon, C., & Disbury, A. (2003). *Understanding organizational context: Inside and outside organizations.* London: Financial Times/Prentice-Hall.

Leigh, D. (2006). SWOT analysis. In J. A. Pershing (Ed.), *Handbook of human performance technology: Principles practices potential* (3rd ed.). San Francisco, CA: Pfeiffer.

Materials Needed

- Flip chart, blackboard, whiteboard, or computer screen that can be used to lead the group through the process
- Markers
- Handouts
- Flip charts positioned around the room for small group use if more than 10 participants

Advantages

Works similarly to brainstorming to get all ideas on the table, but the process is more structured and looks at both internal issues (strengths and weaknesses) and external factors (opportunities and threats). In today's changing economy, a consideration of external factors is critical.

Disadvantages

Is sometimes criticized for a focus on negative factors, but this may reflect a problem with the process followed by the group rather than an issue with the technique itself.

Another criticism is lack of focus on cost and benefits of possible solutions.

Suggestions/Comments

Group members should come to the session prepared to discuss these four areas. Advance explanation of the process and a definition of the terms will help the session move quickly through preliminary steps and allow time to concentrate on discussions that flow from the issues identified. Depending on the situation, you might want to have group members send SWOT factors to you so that you can present the group with a preliminary list. You can have each person do this individually, or you could follow a Delphi process as described in Chapter 13. Involving external stakeholders can increase the information available for planning.

Explanation of SWOT Terms

Strength: an internal competence, valuable resource, or attribute that an organization can use to pursue opportunities in the external environment

Weakness: an internal lack of a competence, resource, or attribute that an organization requires to perform in the external environment

Opportunity: an external possibility that an organization can pursue to gain benefit

Threat: an external factor that has the potential to reduce an organization's performance

Steps

1. Identify stakeholders who are involved in the desired end result.

2. Generate SWOTs.

3. Categorize SWOTs.

4. Deliberate on ways in which the group can:
    - build upon Strengths (what we have),
    - eliminate or reduce Weaknesses (what we lack),
    - exploit Opportunities (what we could gain), and
    - mitigate the effects of Threats (what we could lose).

A conventional SWOT Matrix is presented in Figure 14-1.

Strengths	Weaknesses
• • •	• • •
Opportunities	**Threats**
• • •	• • •

Figure 14-1. SWOT Matrix

The second technique, appreciative inquiry (AI), is a "cooperative search for the best in people, their organizations, and the world around them" (Cooperrider & Whitney, 1999, p. 10). AI is not a traditional problem-solving method of inquiry.

225

Rather, it attempts to redesign the organization by changing the questions that are asked. AI is commonly used in Organization Development; here I discuss AI as it relates to strategic planning.

Focus on Possibilities

Appreciative Inquiry

Name and Description

Appreciative inquiry (AI), an adaptation of action research developed by David Cooperrider and Suresh Srivastava in the 1980s, is an approach for organizational change that focuses on both inquiry and the positive aspects of an organization. The underlying principle is that the way we talk about a system—the stories we tell—can change the system. AI generally pursues a 4-D Cycle consisting of discovery, dream, design, and destiny phases.

References

Cooperrider, D. L. & Whitney, D. (2005). *Appreciative inquiry: A positive revolution in change.* San Francisco, CA: Berrett-Koehler.

Cooperrider, D. L., Whitney, D., & Stavros, J. M. (2008). *Appreciative inquiry handbook* (2nd ed.). Brunswich, OH: Crown Custom and San Francisco, CA: Berrett-Koehler.

Use

When a positive inquiry-based approach is desired, appreciated, and supported by the group and the organization. When participants are willing to use a creative, outside-the-box approach. Aspects of AI can also be used to start any session with a focus on positive news and events, although this captures only a small piece of the process.

Materials Needed

- Flip chart, blackboard, whiteboard, or computer screen that can be used to lead the group through the process
- Markers
- Handouts
- If interviews are conducted, additional space is needed
- Flip charts positioned around the room for small group use
- Recorders for use in collecting stories

Advantages

Participants will have a chance to view things from a different perspective. Reduces the negativity that sometimes occurs with strategic planning. Encourages workers to find a sense of fulfillment in their work. Helps develop a collaborative climate and a sense of ownership in the group or unit.

Disadvantages

Does not have the immediate action steps that occur in several other techniques. In initial stages, may appear that nothing is happening. Some may criticize the lack of problem focus.

Comments/Suggestions

Advance planning is needed. Distribute materials that explain the process and ask for feedback from group members. Provide examples for each stage of the model.

Sample 4D Model	
Discovery:	What gives life?
Dream:	What might be?
Design:	How can it be?
Destiny:	What will be?

The 4D Model is displayed in Figure 14-2.

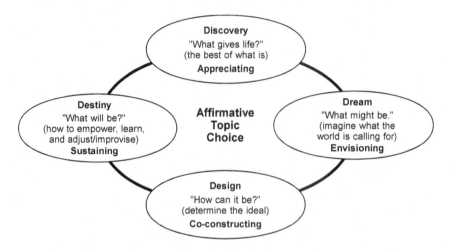

Figure 14-2. Appreciative Inquiry 4D Model

Source: Watkins, J., & Stavros, J. (2009). Appreciative inquiry: OD in the post-modern age. In W. Rothwell, J. Stavros, & R. Sullivan, *Practicing organization development: A guide for leading change.* San Francisco, CA: Jossey-Bass, p. 171. Used with permission.

Steps in Process Adapted for Strategic Planning

Discover: Participants work in dyads or small groups to elicit positive stories about the group and the workplace. Members can interview each other before or during a group session. Possible questions include

- Can you tell me about a positive experience you have had at work?

- What is an example of a time when you were engaged in a project and happy to get to work?

- What do you like most about your work? Your work unit? Your organization?

Dream: The facilitator works with group members to locate themes in stories. This may happen during or outside a session. Session might start with potential themes that are then further developed in the group.

Design: Members create shared images for what they would like the future to be.

Destiny: Group develops creative strategies for putting into practice what was developed in earlier phases and empowering group members to help dreams become practice.

The third technique fits in well with an earlier chapter on creativity and the discussions throughout the book on the importance of working with uncertainty.

Focus on Uncertainty

Our first technique, SWOT, focuses on an analysis of internal and external factors affecting an organization. The second technique, AI, focuses on possibilities and encourages group members to visualize what might be. The third technique, scenario planning, presented below offers another alternative. This technique involves the construction of stories that present alternative versions of what might happen.

Scenario Planning

Name and Description

Scenario planning in its current format was developed by Pierre Wack when he was head of long-range planning at Royal Dutch/Shell during the 1970s and evolved from the "think the unthinkable" research in the 1950s conducted by Herman Kahn. This technique makes use of multiple scenarios or stories of different futures to emphasize the fact that the future is unpredictable and inherently filled with uncertainty. Utilizes and requires substantial amount of information on group and organizational history in order to construct realistic scenarios.

References

Wack, P. (1985). Shooting the rapids. *Harvard Business Review, 63*(6), 139–150.

Chermack, T. J., Badwell, W., & Glick, M. (2010). Two strategies for leveraging teams toward organizational effectiveness: Scenario planning and organizational ambidexterity. *Advances in Developing Human Resources, 12*(1), 137–156.

Materials Needed

- Flip chart, blackboard, whiteboard, or computer screen that can be used to lead the group through the process
- Markers
- Handouts
- Flip charts positioned around the room for small group use if more than 10 participants

Use

To help shift thinking and focus attention on a variety of ways in which the future might unfold

Advantages

Is realistic in terms of the uncertainty imbedded in any planning process and highly relevant to each group or organization since scenarios are developed from data collected from stakeholders.

Disadvantages

Time consuming. Requires considerable information and commitment. The facilitator in concert with group members needs to provide motivation throughout the process to prevent dropouts.

Comments/Suggestions

Advance work is critical. Be sure that participants realize what is involved in this process. Distributing materials on how this technique has been used effectively and ways in which the group and organization will benefit is time well spent.

Steps

Scenario planning involves several steps and a series of group meetings:

1. Perform an analysis prior to the first group session.

2. In group, brainstorm on issues the group/organization is facing.

3. Also in group, rank the factors (1) according to their potential impact on the strategic plan and (2) on their perceived level of uncertainty.

4. At this point, a scenario planning team takes over for a large group and chooses issues that rank high on both impact and uncertainty to use for scenario development. In smaller groups, everyone serves on the team. Each scenario is heavily researched and developed to meet three criteria: plausibility, relevance, and substantial challenge.

5. Scenarios combine variables in interesting ways that provoke deep thought and reflection.

6. The planning team calls further group meetings to develop and discuss scenarios.

7. Scenarios are presented and discussed with stakeholders.

After reading through these three methods for strategic planning, you can see that each has strengths and weaknesses. SWOT is the most traditional of the three and most likely to be known by group members. The AI process evokes strong feelings. People who have experienced AI may become strong advocates, or they may believe that the process is overly optimistic. Scenario planning has been used less in strategic planning so you might have a blank slate in terms of member's perceptions and expectations. See Chermack, Lynham, and Ruona (2001) for more information on scenario planning.

An individual or group opinion of a particular technique is formed in great measure by past experiences. If a prior experience was negative, even if the technique itself was not at fault, that perception will carry forward to the current experience. Advance preparation in terms of distributing a tentative plan and giving participants an opportunity to provide feedback is crucial before any strategic planning session. If you receive negative comments on any aspect of your approach, respond and explain how you will satisfy their concerns. Invite suggestions and adapt as necessary to garner commitment from the group. As we leave this chapter, reflection on group goal setting is useful.

Group Goal Setting

A group goal is a desired result that the group hopes to achieve. For short-term groups, this may be the stated purpose of the group—what it hopes to accomplish. For long-term groups, these goals may be multifaceted and reflect both current and long-term priorities. For the latter groups, goal setting may stand alone as a process or be part of an overall strategic plan. Either way, an assessment of goals is a useful activity. The following statements, adapted from Albanese, Franklin, and Wright (1997, p. 159), can be used by groups to assess both their goals and the goal-setting process:

1. We commit time, energy, and resources to goal setting.
2. Goals are proactive rather than reactive.
3. Goals are written.
4. We have both long-range and short-term goals.
5. Goals are both realistic and challenging.
6. We review and modify our goals on a regular cycle.

In Chapter 2, I discussed how groups often have unclear goals. It seems appropriate that I close this final chapter with a focus on the importance of goal setting. Having clarity about purpose is essential for accomplishment of that purpose.

Summary

This chapter reviewed strategic planning and goal setting and discussed three techniques that can be used for this purpose: SWOT, appreciative inquiry, and scenario planning. Having goals is at the heart of group work. Much of what we do as facilitators centers on helping groups accomplish their tasks and get along with each other in a cooperative and productive manner while they are going about this work. Strategic planning or some type of focused examination of past accomplishment and future needs or desires is a process that works well with the facilitator's neutral role. Since a facilitator usually is not involved in the content of the group's work product, this neutrality allows for a focus on the process itself.

References

Albanese, R., Franklin, G. M., & Wright, P. (1997). *Management* (rev. ed.). Houston, TX: Dame Publications.

Capon, C., & Disbury, A. (2003). *Understanding organizational context: Inside and outside organizations.* London: Financial Times/Prentice-Hall.

Chermack, T. J., Badwell, W., & Glick, M. (2010). Two strategies for leveraging teams toward organizational effectiveness: Scenario planning and organizational ambidexterity. *Advances in Developing Human Resources, 12*(1), 137–156.

Chermack, T. J., Lynham, S. A., & Ruona, W.E.A. (2001). A review of scenario planning literature. *Futures Research Quarterly, 17*(summer), 7–31.

Cooperrider, D. L., & Whitney, D. (1999). *Appreciative Inquiry.* San Francisco, CA: Koehler Communications.

Cooperrider, D. L. & Whitney, D. (2005). *Appreciative inquiry: A positive revolution in change.* San Francisco, CA: Berrett-Koehler.

Cooperrider, D. L., Whitney, D., & Stavros, J. M. (2008). *Appreciative inquiry handbook* (2nd ed.). Brunswich, OH: Crown Custom and San Francisco, CA: Berrett-Koehler.

Leigh, D. (2006). SWOT analysis. In J. A. Pershing (Ed.), *Handbook of human performance technology: Principles practices potential* (3rd ed.). San Francisco, CA: Pfeiffer.

Schermerhorn, J. R. Jr. (1984). *Management for productivity.* New York: John Wiley & Sons.

Wack, P. (1985). Shooting the rapids. *Harvard Business Review, 63*(6), 139–150.

Watkins J., & Stavros, J. (2009). Appreciative inquiry: OD in the post-modern age. In W. Rothwell, J. Stavros, & R. Sullivan, *Practicing organization development: A guide for leading change* (pp. 158–182). San Francisco, CA: Jossey-Bass.

Appendices

Appendix A: Self-Rating of Facilitator Competencies

Appendix B: Memo of Agreement

Self-Rating of Facilitator Competencies

Part A. **Directions**: For each statement, rate your current competency level using the following scale:

5 Exceptional; this is a definite strength of mine
4 Good; not quite a definite strength but close
3 Sufficient for most circumstances
2 Needs improvement
1 Poor; a weakness

_____ 1. Demonstrates evidence of advance planning and preparation

_____ 2. Completes appropriate follow-up activities as contracted

_____ 3. Listens actively

_____ 4. Paraphrases and summarizes segments of content

_____ 5. Clarifies perspectives in disagreements

_____ 6. Uses questions skillfully

_____ 7. Uses body language and nonverbals effectively

_____ 8. Observes and attends to nonverbals in group

_____ 9. Keeps group focused on issues

_____ 10. Helps groups clarify purpose and establish ground rules

_____ 11. Uses techniques appropriate for task and group

_____ 12. Remains neutral as to task outcome

_____ 13. Adheres to established timeframes

_____ 14. Uses appropriate technology and visual aids

_____ 15. Creates a climate that supports interaction and discussion

_____ 16. Encourages group involvement in, and ownership of, issues/task

_____ 17. Uses humor effectively

_____ 18. Monitors group dynamics

_____ 19. Maintains adherence to ground rules

_____ 20. Provides feedback and encourages process skills

_____ 21. Handles disruptive individual(s) whose behavior is detrimental to the group

_____ 22. Focuses group's attention on substantive issues in conflict

_____ 23. Stimulates small group insights and creativity

Part B. Directions: Now that you have finished your initial self-rating, put an asterisk (*) by those competencies that are most important in your work. Any score of "3" or below in those areas should be your primary concern in any plan to improve your competencies.

Note your areas of strength. Although we want to be competent in all aspects of facilitation, we each have areas in which we excel. Those areas, more than likely, are what groups remember and why we are invited back.

 **Memo of Agreement**

To: Potential client

From: Judith Kolb

Date:

Re: Project kickoff session
            Date of event

This memo summarizes today's discussion and our agreement regarding my facilitation of a project kickoff session to be held for **name of group.** Details follow.

Time and Location. The session will begin at 9:00 a.m. and end at 1:30 p.m. on June 4. We will meet at **location.** Lunch will be served at 12:30.

Participants. Fifteen members listed on the attached sheet will attend. Attendance will be verified by **name of person** on June 2; a revised list will be sent to me at that time. Participants will be asked to indicate hours of attendance if they plan to arrive late or leave early.

Agenda. The agenda that is attached reflects my understanding of the day's events as per our two previous discussions. Please contact me if you see any omissions or have any concerns. **Name** will distribute this agenda to all participants by May 21 and will invite feedback to be sent by May 27. You and I will discuss any suggested changes.

My Role and Fee. I will serve as a neutral process facilitator and, in that role, will keep the group focused on the agenda and encourage expression and discussion of all points of view. My fee for the day will be $xxxx, plus expenses.

Logistics. As per our agreement, I will discuss my equipment and logistics needs with **name.**

I look forward to working with you and with the members of **name of group.**

~ **About the Author** ~

Judith A. Kolb is Associate Professor of Education in the Workforce Education and Development Program at The Pennsylvania State University (University Park Campus). She teaches group and team facilitation and other related courses in the Human Resource Development/Organization Development emphasis of study. Dr. Kolb has over 25 years' experience working with groups and teams in a wide variety of contexts and fields including manufacturing, research and development, utilities, education, medicine, and business. Her articles on teamwork and facilitation have appeared in journals such as *Human Resource Development Quarterly, Small Group Research, Journal of European Industrial Training, Journal of Business Communication, Management Communication Quarterly, Performance Improvement Quarterly,* and *Journal of Creative Behavior.*

Dr. Kolb earned a Ph.D. from the University of Denver in communication with a specialty in small group and applied organizational communication, a M.Ed. from Colorado State University in human resource development, and a B.S. from the University of Missouri in business education. Her background in communication, training, and business provides a useful lens for the study and practice of small group facilitation.

~ Index ~

A

Action research, 226
Active listening, 63–65
  defined, 63
Adjourning, 96
Advance planning, 51–55
  agenda format, 53–54
  appropriate dress, 55
  discussions, 51
  including information on facilitator, 54–55
  preparing agenda and related information, 52
Affective conflict, 149, 150–151
Affiliative constraints, on groups, 32–33
Affinity technique/diagram, 191–193
Agenda
  format, 53–54
  including information on facilitator, 54–55
  keeping group focused and, 88
  preparation of, 52
  reviewing, 82–83
Aggressor role, 117, 118
Agree/disagree statements, 84–85
Agreement, facilitation, 51
  sample memo, 239–240
AI. *See* Appreciative inquiry (AI)
Albanese, R., 155, 232
Ambiguity, celebrating, 165–166
Analysis, techniques focusing on, 223–226
Appreciative inquiry (AI), 89, 183, 225, 226–228, 232
Argument, avoiding group think using constructive, 178–179
Arrival, 82
Assumptions, challenging, 164
Attitudes, 125

243

R